Cyril Ray, born 1908, was a scholar both of Manchester Grammar School and of Jesus College, Oxford, where he read history. He has been a war correspondent for the *Manchester Guardian* and the B.B.C., and a foreign correspondent in Rome and Moscow. He has been 'Atticus' of The London *Sunday Times* and assistant editor of the *Spectator*, and has written military histories, but is best known as a writer on wine.

First winner of the Wine and Food Society's André Simon Prize (for his annual anthology, *The Compleat Imbiber*), first English winner of the Bologna Trophy (for his *The Wines of Italy*), Cyril Ray was founder and first chairman, and is now honorary vice-president, of the Circle of Wine Writers.

Bollinger

By the same author

Scenes and Characters from Surtees (Edited with introduction)

From Algiers to Austria: The History of 78 Division in the Second World War

The Pageant of London

Merry England

Regiment of the Line: The Story of the Lancashire Fusiliers

The Gourmet's Companion (Edited with introduction)

The Compleat Imbiber (Edited annually since 1956)

Best Murder Stories (Edited with introduction)

The Wines of Italy

Morton Shand's A Book of French Wines (Revised and edited)

In a Glass Lightly

Lafite: The Story of Château Lafite-Rothschild (Uniform with this book)

Bollinger

The Story of a Champagne

Cyril Ray

ST. MARTIN'S PRESS
NEW YORK

To

MADAME JACQUES BOLLINGER

Grande Dame de la Champagne

et du Champagne

CONTENTS

vii

ILLUSTRATIONS

ix

Illustrations

NOTE: With the exception of the line drawings of the two types of champagne-bottle top, on page 100, and of the structure of a champagne cork, on page 109, specially executed for this book by Mr Michael Broadbent of Christie's, the chapter-headings and other decorative drawings are from Bertall's *La Vigne: Voyage autour des Vins de France*, as they were for my book on Lafite. Bertall's gay, gossipy book was published in Paris in 1878, and he was gathering his material over the previous years. His drawings—freely used by Vizetelly in his *A History of Champagne* (London, 1882)—give an idea of the manners and modes of those who were drinking Bollinger at the time when it was firmly establishing itself on the English market, just before its first royal appointment in 1884.

Introduction

I CAME later in life to love and, indeed, even to respect champagne than I did to love and respect other wines—to love Moselle, say, and claret, as I do, and to respect white burgundy and madeira. It may be that I had been exposed too much in my salad days to the sort of champagne that might well have been used, indeed, as an ingredient of a salad-dressing—thin, sharp stuff that could soon be felt pricking at the stomach walls. Or, on the other hand, to champagnes that had been so heavily sugared to mask their deficiencies that they tasted unnatural in the mouth and, next morning, ached abominably in the head.

But in the early 1950s, when I was already making some claim in the public prints to be an amateur of wine, I was invited by the hospitable brothers Reuss to join a dining-club that had just been founded to drink, enjoy, and sing the praises of Pol Roger champagne, for which their firm, Dent and Reuss, were (and are) the British agents. It is now with shame and embarrassment that I recall saying, in what must have been an odiously (and, I like to think, uncharacteristically) churlish way, that I was prepared to join their club for the sake of their company, but that I was not much of a champagne-lover.

I was welcomed more courteously than my ungraciousness deserved. At my first luncheon with the Pol Roger Club I was served with a superb bottle of Corton Charlemagne to myself—superb, indeed, for Dent and Reuss also ship the burgundies of Louis Latour—the while my fellow members waxed witty under the benign influence of Pol Roger.

As wise parents with a pig-headed child, my kindly hosts quietly left me, without comment, to come round to civilized behaviour at my own pace. A sip, a glass or so, of what my companions were so evidently appreciating, and eventually I was taking my modest whack of however many magnums were being served. I have been a member of the Pol Roger Club now for the best part of twenty years, and I use the phrase 'best part' qualitatively as well as quantatively: Pol Roger has done much to make the past couple of decades tolerable. Partly it is that I have drunk it so often not among strangers at wedding parties but in the good company of good friends; partly, that I have drunk it more often sitting down, with and (better still) immediately before good food, than standing up in over-heated, over-peopled, hired rooms, washing down with it flabby bits of tinned stuffs glued with gelatine to even flabbier pieces of cold toast. Chiefly, of course, it is that Pol Roger is a very good champagne.

*   *   *

If it is to Pol Roger that I owe my conversion to the most convivial of wines, it is to the house of Moët et Chandon, biggest by far of all the champagne firms, that I owe my introduction to the sweet countryside in which it is grown, and to some of the vast cellars in which it is made.

In 1960, as I have recorded elsewhere,[1] I was invited to assist, to use the French expression, at Mr Khrushchev's visit to the Moët et Chandon cellars. My host was the firm's president, Count Robert-Jean de Vogüé, and through him I met—among many other delightful members of the firm and the family—Patrick Forbes (whom I knew of already as a military historian), later to become managing director of the London house, and author of a remarkable monograph on champagne, from which I have learned much and to which I shall refer later, and Moyra Campbell, too, the then *châtelaine* of Château de Saran, at which Moët et Chandon entertain their friends, where I have stayed frequently during the past decade, imbibing knowledge and good wine, and making it my base for sorties into village, vineyard and cellar.

Between whiles, in London, I was being instructed by Denis Stephens-Clarkson, whose firm, Percy Fox, are the agents for Lanson champagne, and who for a time in those days was chairman of the association of London champagne-shippers. It was from him, largely through a generously planned, studiously objective, series of tastings of the whole range of *grandes marques* champagnes,[2] that I learned that there are a dozen or so very

[1] Cyril Ray, *In a Glass Lightly*, London, 1967, chapter 3.
[2] For the *grandes marques*, see chapter 3.

2

good wines indeed that differ not in quality but in style. And later, also through him, I was privileged to fly to France, in good company, to take part in Lanson's bicentenary celebrations, in 1960; to further my acquaintance with another fine wine; and to meet for the first but by no means for the last time, Victor Lanson and his sons.

It was later, through my association with the Directors' Wine Club, a subsidiary of International Distillers and Vintners, one of whose directors, Geoffrey Hallowes, holds the family agency for Heidsieck Monopole, that I came to know yet another notable champagne, to enjoy in Reims something of the same hospitality already extended to me in Epernay, and to gaze out, with a glass of the firm's pretty pink champagne in my hand, over the rolling vineyards of the Montagne de Reims from the historic windmill that it owns at Verzenay.

*   *   *

All of which leads up to the subject of this book.

The more I met such distinguished makers and shippers of champagne as I have mentioned, the more I travelled in the region, talking to hoteliers and restaurateurs, the more I discussed the wine with knowledgeable merchants and eminent amateurs at home, the more I was brought to realize the very important place that Bollinger holds—or, to be more precise, shares with one other wine—in the respect and affection of the champagne world.

Almost—not quite, but almost—invariably, if I asked the maker or agent of one of the great champagnes what wine he would drink if he did not drink his own, the answer would be either Krug or Bollinger or, often enough, both—bracketed equal, or as alternatives to each other, or either one first with the other a very close second.

It was not that others were never mentioned—as well as those that I have already quoted on my own account, some reference must be made to Roederer and to Veuve Clicquot—but no other was mentioned so often. It was not that whoever it was whom I was questioning held his own wine to be in any way inferior, or that he would wish to disparage any of the other dozen or more great wines of the region. It was simply that these two small but immensely distinguished houses were universally recognized as producing wines of quite outstanding character by sticking stubbornly to traditional methods of vinification and by paying the highest prices for the finest grapes—by always, in short, putting quality first, whatever the cost, in money, in time, in labour or in anxieties.

And in the case of Bollinger, there is the very special regard in which the world of champagne holds Madame Bollinger herself, who succeeded to the control of the family firm on the death of her husband in 1941, and is still, at the age of seventy, very much the full-time working head, having doubled the yearly production of Bollinger in her thirty years' presidency without ever lowering its standards—if anything, by raising them—while remaining, indeed, the most vigorous exponent of traditional methods in the great, though usually good-humoured, debate that continues in the tasting-rooms and over the dinner-tables of Champagne between the traditionalists and the innovators.

How different the picture that formed in my mind's eye, in the course of those ten or a dozen years over which I now look back, from the one projected thirty and forty years before, in the days when I was myself, briefly and ingloriously, a prep-school master, by the unfortunate first couple of pages of the late Evelyn Waugh's first novel!

Mr. Sniggs, the Junior Dean, and Mr. Postlethwaite, the Domestic Bursar, sat alone in Mr. Sniggs' room overlooking the garden quad at Scone College. From the rooms of Sir Alastair Digby-Vaine-Trumpington, two staircases away, came a confused roaring and breaking of glass. They alone of the senior members of Scone were at home that evening, for it was the night of the annual dinner of the Bollinger Club. The others were all scattered over Boar's Hill and North Oxford at gay, contentious little parties, or at other senior common-rooms, or at the meetings of learned societies, for the annual Bollinger dinner is a difficult time for those in authority.

It is not accurate to call this an annual event, because quite often the Club is suspended for some years after each meeting.

There is tradition behind the Bollinger; it numbers reigning kings among its past members. At the last dinner, three years ago, a fox had been brought in in a cage and stoned to death with champagne bottles. What an evening that had been! This was the first meeting since then, and from all over Europe old members had rallied for the occasion. For two days they had been pouring into Oxford: epileptic royalty from their villas of exile; uncouth peers from crumbling country seats; smooth young men of uncertain tastes from embassies and legations; illiterate lairds from wet granite hovels in the Highlands; ambitious young barristers and Conservative candidates torn from the London season and the indelicate advances of debutantes; all that was most sonorous of name and title was there for the beano.

'The fines!' said Mr. Sniggs, gently rubbing his pipe along the side of his nose. 'Oh my! the fines there'll be after this evening!'

There is some highly prized port in the senior common-room cellars that is only brought up when the College fines have reached £50.

'We shall have a week of it at least,' said Mr. Postlethwaite, 'a week of Founder's port.'

A shriller note could now be heard rising from Sir Alastair's rooms; any who have heard that sound will shrink at the recollection of it; it is the sound of the English county families baying for broken glass. Soon they would all be tumbling out into the quad, crimson and roaring in their bottle-green evening coats, for the real romp of the evening.

'Don't you think it might be wiser if we turned out the light?' said Mr. Sniggs.

In darkness the two dons crept to the window. The quad below was a kaleidoscope of dimly discernible faces.

'There must be fifty of them at least,' said Mr. Postlethwaite. 'If only they were all members of the College! Fifty of them at ten pounds each. Oh my!'

'It'll be more if they attack the Chapel,' said Mr. Sniggs. 'Oh, please God, make them attack the Chapel.'

Evelyn Waugh had been down from Oxford not much more

than a year when *Decline and Fall* was published, in 1928, and at Oxford, he has recorded,[3] he was wont to drink a tankard of beer for breakfast and, apart from that, 'we were not discriminating . . . we tried everything we could lay hands on, but table-wines were the least of our interests'.

It is a pity. Champagne is not a hooligan's drink, nor is Bollinger a hooligan's champagne. Had the young Evelyn Waugh paid less attention to drinking Yquem 'in a mood of ostentation', and to Tokay, Bristol Milk, and 'a dark sherry named Brown Bang', and more attention to the subtler charms of champagne—which he never even mentions in the reminiscences that I quote—he would not have applied, merely because of a syllabic similarity, the name of one of the most civilized of wines to even the fictional simulacrum of so philistine a sodality as the Bullingdon.

(Mr Humphrey Lyttelton made kinder use of the name in one of his engaging articles on the splendours and glooms of dining out: 'I find champagne at midday has such a calamitous effect on my working day that I am tempted to coin the word "bollingering", meaning much the same as malingering, only nicer.')

So different, anyway, was my picture of the house of Bollinger from Evelyn Waugh's of the Bollinger Club, baying for broken glass, that when my publisher asked me to follow my little monograph on Lafite[4] with a second book to be similarly not on wine in general, or even on a type of wine, but about one wine in particular, and this time on a great champagne, I knew—after an affectionate backward glance at Pol Roger and Moët, Lanson and Heidsieck Monopole—that my choice was going to be between Krug and Bollinger and that, as between the two, the scale would be tipped by the personality of Madame Bollinger herself, together with the fact that her firm (which is a private company, entirely family-owned) not only makes great wine but owns great vineyards, whereas the house of Krug, which also makes great wine, has few vineyards of its own and, although entirely controlled of course by members of the Krug family, who are majority shareholders, is partly owned by the houses of Cointreau and Rémy-Martin.

[3] 'First Faltering Steps: Drinking', in *Compleat Imbiber*, 6, London, 1963.
[4] Cyril Ray, *Lafite: the Story of Château Lafite-Rothschild*, London, 1968.

Having thus briefly given the reasons for my choice of a subject—reasons which will be amplified, I hope, by much that follows—it is my duty to a great wine and to the great lady who presides over its making (as well as to myself and my publisher) to make clear, as I did in the introduction to my similar work on Château Lafite, that this is in no way a *sponsored* book. It was my publisher who suggested that a book on an individual champagne should follow my book on an individual claret, and it was I who suggested what the individual champagne should be. It was then commissioned by the publisher in the ordinary way of business, and it is in the ordinary way of business that it is now published.

The idea of the book was given the warmest welcome by the firm of Bollinger, and also by Mentzendorff and Co., its London agents, and I have had the greatest possible help from the directors of both firms, and the greatest possible hospitality at Ay while I pursued my researches and asked my endless questions. But nobody at Ay or in London has had any say—except, of course, when I have asked for specific information on matters of fact—in what I should or should not write. Neither the house of Bollinger nor the house of Mentzendorff has paid me a fee. All the opinions expressed are my own—especially when I comment on differences of method between Bollinger and other houses, about whom the Bollinger directors are always extremely complimentary—and although I expect most of those opinions, though perhaps not all, to be shared by the directors of Bollinger and of Mentzendorff, the point is that I have never asked them.

In particular, comparisons of *style* between Bollinger and other champagnes, and between the other champagnes themselves, are entirely my own. I found it impossible—sometimes frustratingly so—to get any Bollinger director even to compare styles, however objectively, let alone to discuss the relative qualities of other champagnes.

* * *

It will already be clear that I owe much, and that this book owes much, to champagne houses other than Bollinger. That this

Bollinger

should be so is typical of Champagne and of its people—particularly of those who make or market the *grandes marques*. For their rivals are their friends; they speak admiringly of each other's wines; and they all welcome the genuine amateur and the enquiring student—some of them with positively princely hospitality—even if the stated purpose of their enquiries is to be a book in praise of a competitor.

So, in addition to the names I have already mentioned, I must acknowledge here my indebtedness to Madame Odette Pol Roger and M. Christian de Billy (and his wife) of Pol Roger; to the Comtesse Lecoîntre, who has succeeded the Hon. Moyra Campbell at Moët et Chandon's Château de Saran, and her colleagues the Comtesse de Maigret, M. Claude Fourman and M. Jean-Paul Médard; MM. Henri Chapman and Henri Wisser of Heidsieck Monopole; M. and Mme André Rouzaud, of the family and of the firm of Roederer; M. and Mme Jean-Charles Heidsieck of the firm of Charles Heidsieck; M. Claude Taittinger; and M. and Mme Jean Lallier of Bollinger's near neighbours, Deutz and Geldermann.

My veteran colleague, the late M. André Simon,[5] and my less aged colleague, Mr Julian Jeffs, have helped me with the loan of rare books; the Senior Meteorological Officer at the London Weather Centre with comparative tables; Colonel Maurice Buckmaster with advice, introductions, hospitality in Champagne, illustrations and statistics. Besides contributing the helpful little line drawings in the text of Chapter 6, Mr Michael Broadbent of Christie's has told me much about the taste for old champagne. I always learn something about wine that I did not know before when I meet Mr Edmund Penning-Rowsell, or read his work. Here, I must make especial mention of a series of articles on champagne that he contributed to *The Financial Times* during April and May 1965. M. J. Dargent and Colonel Bonal, of the Comité Interprofessionel du Vin de Champagne, at Epernay, have been patient under questioning and hospitable at table; and,

[5] André Simon died as this book was going to press, well into his ninety-fourth year. If references to him in later pages read as though he were still alive, that, after all, is how he seems to those of us who knew and worked with him.

8

as before, I must express my gratitude for research undertaken by Mrs Joan St George Saunders, of Writer's and Speaker's Research, and for the enthusiastic support of my friend and publisher, Mr Derek Priestley, of Peter Davies. The quotation from Evelyn Waugh in this introduction is by kind permission of Messrs A. D. Peters and Co. My secretary, Miss Jennifer Higgie, has typed, retyped and typed again, declining the appropriate fortifying draughts of Bollinger lest she find my cramped handwriting more difficult even than usual to decipher.

Chiefly, though, my thanks are due to Madame Bollinger herself, president of the house of Bollinger, and to her fellow directors, MM. Claude d'Hautefeuille, Yves Moret de Rocheprise and Christian Bizot, for much patient guidance in cellar, vineyard and among documents; to their wives for delightful hospitality; and to M. Guy Adam, the *chef de cave*, for skilfully arranged tastings. In London, the directors of Mentzendorff, the house which for well over a century has been Bollinger's British agent, have been enthusiastically encouraging: I refer to Messrs Leslie Seyd, Anthony Leschallas, Michael Druitt, and John McNally.

*   *   *

I must make it clear that I have tried to summarize the complicated methods by which champagne is made, rather than go into technical detail. Such parts of the cellar processes as I have brought into rather sharper focus are those in which the practice at Bollinger differs from that at other cellars: this is a book about Bollinger, not about champagne in general, and certainly not about how to make it.

I have been even more summary about vineyard and vine. The grape is grown the same way in this vineyard and in that: the laws of *appellation* make this obligatory. Bollinger differs from other champagnes—not all other, but most other—not in the way its grapes are grown in the vineyard, as it differs in the way its wine is actually made in the cellar, but in the grading of its own vineyards, and of those it buys from. It is this, therefore, that I have dwelt upon.

Those who wish to study more closely the whole champagne-making process and the cycle of work in the vineyards must be referred to Patrick Forbes's monumental *Champagne: the Wine, the Land and the People*—the most detailed account ever written, or ever likely to be, of how a particular type of wine is made, as well as a classic guide to the countryside and its customs. Visitors to the region should not drive a mile without it: I never do.

On the other hand, I have devoted what some may consider a disproportionate amount of space to the riots of 1911, compared with that given to the rest of the history of champagne. This is because I think that they and their importance in bringing about much-needed reforms have been dismissed too summarily in most other books about champagne, perhaps even in Mr Forbes's; because the most violent disturbance was in Bollinger's own town of Ay; and because of the significance that Bollinger attach to their premises' having been spared by the rioters.

* * *

There have been few enough readers of my previous works, but some such may discover in chapter 9 comments on and quotations relevant to the various types of champagne glass that appeared a few years ago, pretty well word for word the same, in the chapter 'Beaded Bubbles' in my little book, *In a Glass Lightly*. I have taken a passage from that same chapter to illustrate the change of taste in France from sweet to dry champagne. I also quote an observation made by the barman of the Gritti Palace Hotel, Venice, in the same words I used in an article in *Compleat Imbiber*, 10. There are a couple of other briefer passages in which I have plagiarized myself.

I make no apology, but am prepared to offer an explanation: I expressed myself, in those previous pieces, as clearly and as well as I knew how, and I see no reason why I should make myself less clear, and my prose perhaps even less elegant, by varying three or four brief passages merely for variation's sake.

* * *

A word about words.

In writing about a product made in France by Frenchmen it is all too easy to pockmark every page with italics. To avoid this, I have left unitalicized such French words as are well understood by all English-speakers who are interested in wine, but for which there is no English equivalent. (Vigneron is the obvious example: 'vine-dresser' seems disturbingly archaic, and Mr Edward Hyams's 'vinearoon' has never commended itself to me—or, it would seem, to anyone else.) It is impossible to be entirely logical if one is italicizing some foreign words and not others, and I hope those readers will forgive me who would have done it differently themselves.

As I wrote this book, it seemed natural to use 'Bollinger' with a singular form of the verb when discussing the wine—'Bollinger is a dry, full-bodied wine'—and with a plural form when referring to the firm: 'Bollinger own vineyards in Ay.' I hope it comes as naturally to the reader.

Finally, the pronunciation of the name.

Although, as will be seen, Bollinger was originally a German name, it is never now pronounced in the German way: the 'g' is invariably soft. Moreover, members of the family and of the firm do not find it either difficult or anomalous to pronounce the name in the French way when in France and in the English way when in England. Or even, when speaking English, to use both pronunciations in the same sentence—the French when referring to the family, the English when to the wine. And I should certainly consider it as affected, when ordering a bottle in an English restaurant, to pronounce Bollinger as anything but an ordinary English word.

I wish only that I found myself pronouncing it more often.

1. La Champagne

La Champagne, feminine, is the region: *le champagne* is the wine, masculine because it is *le vin de la Champagne*.

From this point on we cease to italicize words that are as English now as they are French, but we shall distinguish between the place and its product by using a capital initial for the one, lower case for the other.

In the strict laws of *appellation* that govern the making and the naming of French wines, the word 'champagne' has a very precise and jealously guarded meaning, but as a place name 'La Champagne' has no more of an official status in France than 'Wessex' or 'Mercia' or 'Northumbria' has in England.

What had been in the Middle Ages an independent county, ruled by the counts of Champagne, and from 1286 a province of the kingdom of France, was split up at the Revolution into *départements*, just as the other historic provinces were—Picardy, Normandy, Brittany, Burgundy and the rest. 'La Champagne' is now the general and unofficial, but historic and evocative term for a region consisting of the four *départements*, Ardennes, Marne, Aube and Haute Marne, extending in that order, north to south, from the Belgian frontier to the north-eastern corner of Burgundy

—itself once an independent grand duchy, then a province of France, and now, in precisely the same way as Champagne, a region that has no official existence, but that gives its historic name to a world-famous wine.

The Champagne we are concerned with here, though, is far smaller than the ancient province. It is *la Champagne viticole*, the Champagne wine-growing region, lying almost entirely in the *département* of Marne—slightly less than 40,000 acres[1] of vine-yards. This region consists of three contiguous parts. One is spread over the slopes of the Montagne, so-called, de Reims, a system of chalk downs immediately south of Reims, a mere six hundred feet above the surrounding countryside, and at most nine hundred feet above sea level, stretching for a dozen miles east to west, and facing south.

Then, nine miles or so of the Vallée de la Marne vineyards, also facing south, across the river, from Tours sur Marne in the east to Cumières in the west; and the Côte des Blancs, running south for a dozen miles or so from Epernay and facing east.

These three component parts of one compact region form on the map a rather flattened question mark, with the Montagne de Reims and the Vallée de la Marne vineyards curving round towards, and meeting each other, in the east to form the reversed C, and the Côte des Blancs running south to form the vertical.

This smoothly undulating downland country is part of the same chalk system as that of Kent and Sussex, with much the same characteristics of scenery and climate. (Even its people have much the same cut of the jib as their neighbours across the Channel.) Indeed, this is Britain's nearest wine-growing area—well under a couple of hundred miles south-east of Dover as the crow flies.

What is more, it is the northernmost wine-growing region of France and, save for the Moselle and the less important reaches of the Rhine, the most northerly in the world.

[1] Out of 42,340 acres under vines legally entitled at the end of 1969 to the *appellation* 'champagne'. There are outlying patches, very small and—so far as the finest champagnes are concerned—unimportant, west along the Marne towards Paris, and south-east, along the upper reaches of the Marne and the Aube, beyond Troyes.

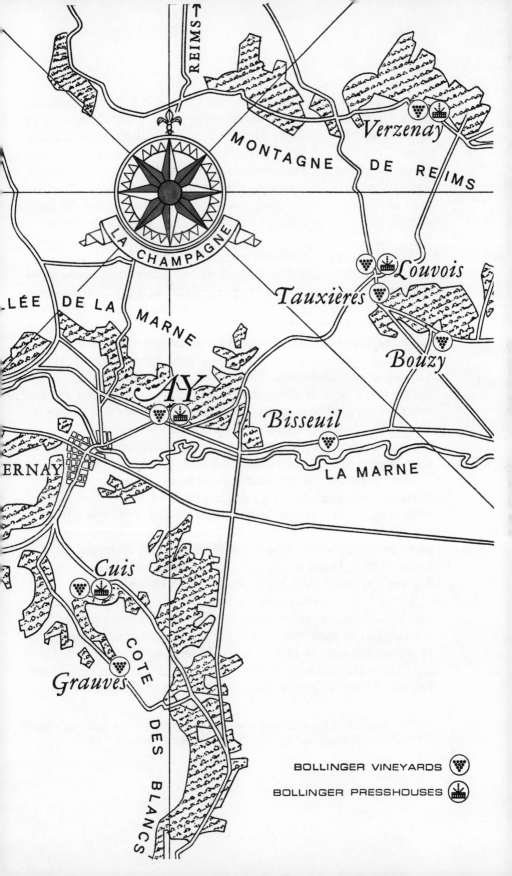

It is generally agreed that 50 degrees north is the northerly limit for viticulture, give or take a few miles for differences of altitude and for specially favoured or particularly unfavourable sites. This line of latitude runs, as near as makes no matter, through Mainz, at the confluence of the Rhine and the Main, across the southernmost tip of Belgium, cutting the French coast near Dieppe and the English coast at the Lizard. Reims, the main city of our wine-growing Champagne, lies less than a degree to the south.[2]

This temperate northern region of chalk downs and river valleys has the same feel as well as the same look about it as the related region of south-eastern England. Lying, as it does, in the continental land mass, farther from the sea than the North and the South Downs, it may be a very little warmer in the summer than Kent and Sussex, a very little colder in the winter—but very little warmer or colder. There may be a little less rainfall over the year—but very little less. There is usually a little more sunshine —and it is this little more that makes it a wine-growing region, where Kent and Sussex are not. But the weather is as fickle as England's, and the hours of sunshine can sometimes be pretty well as inadequate, which is why there are vintage years in champagne, non-vintage years, and years that are disastrous.

It is a country of misty mornings and of cool evenings, of wide horizons bounded by hog's-back ridges of low hills bristling with woods, of shallow green valleys laced with the silver of slow-moving rivers, of grey steeples and quiet villages—a region often swept by wind, where snow and hail are frequent enough in the winter, frosts in the spring, but where on a still summer's day the fine chalk dust hangs in the air to soften every prospect.

The woods are of oak and beech; birch, ash and chestnut. In this part of France, at any rate, the French have been kinder than the English to their countryside, and refrained from placing rectangular plantations of conifers where conifers do not belong. All that an Englishman would find exotic about these woods and forests of Champagne is that grunting and snuffling in them are

[2] See Appendix I for a climatic comparison between Reims and Tunbridge Wells: Reims is about 49° 25′ N., Tunbridge Wells about 51° 21′ N.

wild boar and their young, ranging adventurously westward from the Ardennes and in graver danger than they know of ending up as *sanglier* and as *marcassin*, respectively, on the menus of starred restaurants in Reims and Epernay and Fère-en-Tardenois.

The little grey villages are puritanically quiet. Some have little to say to the motorist driving through, but some are bright with climbing roses in the early summer, when there are cornflowers and poppies in the cornfields, and the fields of mustard are a dazzling yellow. This is mustard as well as champagne country—champagne-mustard country, indeed, for a sharp pale mustard, not unlike English mustard, is made from the local crop and the local wine in Magenta, a suburb of Epernay, sold in every shop and served in every restaurant in the region in pots the shape of champagne bottles. (The *appellation* laws for champagne are so strict that the maker is forbidden to state on his label, in any language, that his product is made of mustard and champagne. It has to be *moutarde au vin provenant de la Champagne*: made from 'mustard seed, wine from Champagne district'. The name 'champagne', by itself, is reserved for the sparkling wine, made in the approved way, from the approved grapes, pruned in the approved way, gathered at the approved time, from vineyards in the approved areas, and may not be used on a mustard pot, or even a bottle of the still wine of the region, which may only be styled, *'vin nature de la Champagne'*, lest unscrupulous foreigners pump bubbles into it and claim it as champagne.)

* * *

Once, long ago, after my first visit, I wrote that this was a dull countryside. (I had come to it from the dizzily steep vineyards that look down on some of the more dramatically handsome stretches of the Rhine.) Now that I know it well, I know that it is gently beautiful.

All that makes it look different from the downland country that lies on either side of my own Kentish Weald is the vineyards —great sweeps and rolling billows of deep-green corduroy in high summer, when the vines are in full leaf, red and bronze and gold in the autumn, and, in the winter, the vines' metal supports making a million black verticals against the snow.

Reims is just beyond the northern edge of this region but is, as it were, its capital, a busy shopping centre as well as a cathedral and, far more recently, a university city.

With a population of 160,000 or so, it is about as big as out-of-season Brighton, say, or as Middlesbrough, but by French standards this makes it relatively bigger and more important—seventeenth in size of the cities of France.

There is a superb cathedral, coronation place for a thousand years of the kings of France (and the even more interesting, to my mind, Basilique St Remi); there are the *son et lumiere* and the museums; there are too the departmental stores and cafes and souvenir shops. Yet Reims is as provincial in its outlook and its cultural amenities as any English town of the same size.

For Paris is a mere hundred miles away, and the most cultivated and the most worldly Champagne families keep apartments there, the younger members boasting of how much less than two hours they take on the N.3 in their Citroëns or their flash foreign cars. It is in Paris that they have their clothes made and their hair dressed, do their entertaining and their theatre-going. Reims would be a more lordly place were it twice as far from the capital.

Because, though, this is an age of gadding about for pleasure as well as for profit; because the relatives are still alive of Americans who fought and died in these parts in two world wars; because of travel supplements in the Sunday papers and because of package tours—for these and a score of other reasons it is no longer true as it was when Robert Tomes, who had been United States consul in Reims, wrote in 1867 that his countrymen, 'are so fond of hiving within the luxurious delights of Paris . . . that they care not to wander, even for a moment, from the lustfulness of the French capital, or the publicity of the European highways. It is thus that Rheims, with no incitement to expense and no occasion for display, is generally unheeded by the profuse and ostentatious American traveller.' Today's American traveller may not be so profuse or so ostentatious as the traveller of 1867, but he leaves precious little unheeded: certainly not Reims.

I doubt if it was true that when Mr Tomes spent his two tut-tutting years at the Lion d'Or the city's 'young working females, almost without exception, added to what they received for labor the wages of sin', or that their parents shared 'the proceeds of the double career of infamy and industry of their daughters', and, although I have made no first-hand investigations, I am sure that it is not true now.

Mr Tomes's 'young working females' of a century ago were employed in the woollen mills: Reims has never been, and is not now, wholly given over to champagne. To this day, according to Mr Patrick Forbes, the old woollen families regard the champagne magnates as parvenus, no matter how noble their names.

All the same, no fewer than thirty-seven champagne houses have Reims as their headquarters, storing their millions of bottles in the scores of miles of cellars—developed, no doubt, from the caverns dug in search of building materials for the Roman and the medieval city, and the great cathedral

There are precisely as many other great champagne houses, though, in Epernay, which has less than a fifth the population of Reims and is very much a small country town so far as its amenities go. But with the vineyards pressing more obviously close to the edge of the town than they do to the edge of Reims; with its great Avenue de Champagne, lined on either side with the splendid headquarters of one famous house after another—among them the biggest, Moët et Chandon, and another vast organization, Mercier; and with the offices there of the governing body of the trade, the Comité Interprofessionel du Vin de Champagne, the *sparnaciens* regard their town as being more particularly the champagne capital than is Reims. And with some justice.

What, then, are we to say about tiny Ay?

Epernay is a fifth the size of Reims, and Ay is a quarter the size of Epernay—and only a couple of miles away, on the other side of the river and the canal.

One would call it a big village rather than a small country town were it not for the size of the houses in which Ay's great champagne families have lived for generations, and the importance and the long history of their firms—among them Ayala; that fine, old-fashioned firm, Deutz and Geldermann; and, most famous of all, Bollinger.

One might think of it even as a suburb of Epernay, save that it is older and was once of far greater importance—so much so that *agéens* believe that towns and villages in the immediate neighbourhood are named according to their geographical relationship to Ay: if you travel from Reims, then Avenay is *avant Ay*, Verzenay and Verzy are *vers Ay*, and Epernay is known to the guide-books and the map-makers, they say, only because it is *après Ay*.

This may not be etymologically correct, but it is not bigheaded of these small-town people to believe it: it will be seen in a later chapter how, for a thousand years of so, it is so often 'the wines of Ay' that are referred to—far more frequently than any other of the wines of the region, such as Sillery and Bouzy, Hautvillers and Avize. It was seldom, in the old days, 'the wines of Champagne', hardly ever 'the wines of Reims' or of Epernay.

Ay was the heart of the region, and almost as much its capital as Reims.

Partly, no doubt, this was because of the place's strategic importance, guarding the way from the north and east into the valley of the Marne. But at least as much because of the importance of the vineyards climbing from the very edge of the town to the wooded crest of hills behind, and facing due south, so that the Pinot Noir grape here ripens early and reaches a perfection of maturity that it often falls marginally short of elsewhere. For as long as there have been written records, back to the time of still red and pink wines, these grapes have produced the noblest wines of the region—for so long, indeed, that there is evidence that almost nine hundred years ago Pope Urban II declared that there was no better wine in the world than that of Ay. Admittedly, Pope Urban II was a *champenois*. (Indeed Mr Patrick Forbes has suggested that this was why the noblemen of the region responded so much more enthusiastically than those elsewhere to his appeal for the Second Crusade.) But it was the wines of Ay especially that His Holiness commended, not those of Champagne in general.

Since the region first devoted itself to sparkling wine, Ay has proved the only exception to the rule that champagne *must* be blended, as 'the produce of most of Champagne districts lacks charm in its individual loneliness . . . the highest excellence demands a blending of wine from various localities', whereas the wine of Ay 'comes nearest to the ideal type of Champagne, which every blender makes his goal, and it is indeed . . . the only wine that unblended gives a more or less satisfactory Champagne in the modern acceptation of the term. Avize produces a wine of surpassing delicacy, but it needs the mixture of the wines of the Mountain, which provide body and generosity. Verzenay is specially renowned for vinosity combined with freshness, Bouzy for velvety softness, Ambonnay for fragrance, Cramant for *finesse*, Avize for subtle shades of taste and Ay for bouquet.'[3]

Ay again: this time for the fragrance, as well as for the completeness of its wine.

Today, this tiny, sleepy town houses the headquarters of no fewer than eighteen champagne firms—admittedly, some of these are very small, but the total is more than any other place in the region save Reims and Epernay, and they are not vineyard towns, as Ay is. Put another way, it is perhaps even more impressive: Ay is one-twentieth the size of Reims, but houses half as many champagne firms. Count up the rows of vines that stretch along the Châlons road and up the slopes; then the bottles and the magnums in the cellars that have been tunnelled in the chalk— some of them in Roman times—and marvel that so small a place could be so rich. Small wonder that the *portail* of Ay's sixteenth-century church of St Brice—much of it, though not the work of which I write, over-restored even before the damage of the last war—is deeply carved with a motif of the vine and its fruit. Ay has good reason to thank God for the grape.

The houses of the champagne families of Ay hide themselves and their courtyards behind high walls, and the more modest dwellings of vignerons and cellar-workers, shop-keepers and clerks also present blank faces to the passer-by. There are no gardens and no window-boxes, as there are at Hautvillers only a couple of miles away, a self-consciously pretty village, with some claim, as will be seen later, to being the birthplace of champagne.

So the little town, straggling along between the southward-facing slopes of the Montagne de Reims and the poplar-lined

---

[3] H. Warner Allen, *White Wines and Cognac*, London, 1952.

canal, is not at all picturesque, not at all pretty: there is a sleepy, shuttered look about it, as though it were always Sunday afternoon.

Yet this is so much, and has been for so long, the heart-town of *La Champagne viticole* that there is one family still living in Ay that have been wine-growers, father to son in direct line, since the thirteenth century. To make a jump to relatively modern times, many have been there since the eighteenth: as will be seen in chapter 4, the firm of Bollinger was established in 1829 to ship wines from vineyards acquired by the forebears of the first Madame Bollinger something like a century before.

I Bollinger vineyards under snow: typical Champagne country sweeps away to the horizon.

II The *portail* of the 16th-century church of St Brice at Ay. Cherubs shown tending the black and white grapes.

2. Le Champagne

THE Romans set their mark on Champagne: Reims was a great Roman city—the Athens of Gaul, said the Emperor Hadrian—as the Porte de Mars bears witness to this day.

Recent researches, though, have cast doubt on what serious historians of viticulture had long maintained: that it was the Romans who brought the culture of the vine and the craft of wine-making to the region. Mr Patrick Forbes has declared roundly that the much-quoted '*caetera Galliae vina, sunt Regalibus menses expedita e Campania Remense et quod vin d'Ai vocant*',[1] attributed to Pliny the Elder, and referred to even by the scholarly André Simon, is an invention, and Mr Edward Hyams states that 'the youngest vineyard of France is almost certainly that of Champagne'.[2] Mr Hyams declares that it is younger than that of the Loire in general—even of the Nantaise—and adds that, 'like Alsace, Champagne has no significance for the diffusion of the vine: for it was a backwater, filled up long after the main-stream of viticulture had flowed further north'.

[1] 'Are the other wines of Gaul, picked for the table of the king, not in fact those of the *campagna* of Reims, and that called the wine of Ay?'
[2] Edward Hyams, *Dionysus: a Social History of the Wine Vine*, London, 1965.

True, we know that the wild vine flourished in Champagne long before the Romans came to Reims, for fossilized vine-leaves have been found near Epernay embedded in chalk of the Tertiary period.

But there is no evidence that the Gauls of Roman times or before ever cultivated these vines, or made wine from their wild grapes, and it seems certain now that the legionaries' ration was of Italian, Spanish or Provençal wine. The law of A.D. 92 by which the Emperor Domitian—whether under the influence of the Italian wine-growers' lobby, or because of the shortage of wheat—forbade the production of wine in the military provinces of the Empire was never fully implemented in the more fully developed wine-growing areas, such as the Gironde and the Rhône, Provence and Burgundy, but Champagne offered a less obviously suitable climate; forests would have had to be cleared for vineyards to be planted; and if a modest beginning had, in fact, been made in the way of viticulture, which seems doubtful, Domitian's law would have been enough to stifle it at birth.

All the same, when Mr Hyams refers to Champagne as the youngest vineyard in France, we must remember that the standards of vineyard age in that blessed country are pretty formidable: Champagne as a vineyard is something like fifteen hundred years old.

We know at any rate that when St Rémi, the first Archbishop of Reims, died in A.D. 530, he left vineyards in his will; there are references in monastic and church records of the eighth and ninth centuries A.D. to the wines of the region—even to wines specifically from the Montagne de Reims and from the *rivière*, which is to say from the Valleé de la Marne vineyards.

For a thousand years, the church and the monasteries cultivated and extended the vineyards, constantly improving the methods of wine-making. By A.D. 1200, according to André Simon, Henri d'Andelys could refer in his book, *Bataille des Vins*, to the wines of Reims, Epernay and Hautvillers as among the best of France; a century earlier, Pope Urban II, as already noted, had declared that it was the wine of Ay that was best.

A later pope, Leo X, is said to have had a Champagne vineyard of his own: at any rate, there is a strip of vines on the right of the road from Damery to Ay that is called Le Léon to this day, and the locals will tell you that this was Pope Leo's.

For that matter, Leo X's great contemporary Renaissance princes, the Emperor Charles V, Francis I of France, and our own Henry VIII, are all said to have owned vineyards and presses in Champagne or, according to another version, to have kept their own agents or brokers there, to buy them the best. There seems to be no written evidence for this, but it is interesting that it should be believed, and what at any rate is true is that a French admiral, Bonnivet, sent Ay wine to Wolsey in 1518; and that Francis I, having tasted the same breed of wine when he visited Châlons-sur-Marne in 1535, asked for more in 1537, to stock his royal palaces, against a visit from the Hungarian queen-mother.

If Francis I thought highly of the wine of Ay, Henri IV, who came to the throne in 1589, proclaimed it quite positively as his favourite. This although he himself had been born as far away from Champagne as a man could be, and still be a Frenchman— in Béarn, at the foot of the Pyrenees, in the Basque country—and had had his infant lips taken from his mother's breast for them to be sprinkled with the wine of Jurançon, from just outside Pau.

To be sure, Morton Shand wrote that Henri 'blessed every wine of France with a sagacious and exclusive preference',[3] but his pleasure in the wines of Ay and his introduction of them to court is well-attested, and it may well be that his close friendship with Brulart de Sillery, his chancellor, who inherited vast estates of vineyards on the Montagne de Reims, and a coat-of-arms blazoned with casks entwined by vines, had much to do with his continued patronage. It may well be, too, that if it was the wine of Jurançon that got *le vert galant* off to a good start, it was the wine of Ay that kept his gallantry green.

What sort of wine was it that now began to spread across France the name and fame of Champagne?

First of all, it was not yet a fully sparkling wine, though it nearly always showed a tendency to sparkle in the spring after the vintage: grapes grown in a cool climate ferment slowly, and fermentation is often not complete when winter comes. As the

[3] Morton Shand, *A Book of French Wines*, revised and edited by Cyril Ray, London, 1964.

temperature rises again in the spring, fermentation begins again
—this is the secondary fermentation, which will of itself give a
wine a greater or a lesser degree of prickle or *pétillance*. Once it
can be induced, encouraged and controlled, as the *champenois*
eventually learned how to do, a fully sparkling wine is possible.

Nor, at this time, was champagne the clear and limpid 'white'
or, more precisely, pale gold, of today. Nowadays, at least two-
thirds of the vineyards of Champagne are planted with black
grapes—with the Pinot Noir of nearby Burgundy—and let us
reasonably assume that Champagne may well, in those days, have
been largely a black-grape country, even if the grapes were not
the classic grapes of today. But this does not mean that all the
wine was red: there is not usually enough sun in so northern a
climate as that of Champagne to ripen black grapes to the richness required in the skins for red wines, as made in those days.
Better varieties of vine, and improved methods both of viticulture and of vinification would have to be discovered before it
was possible to produce truly red champagnes at all consistently.

So all the wine of the country was still, or only slightly
pétillant, and that for a short time, and what was not red, which
meant most of it, was probably not quite white, either, but with
something of a tinge, or a certain murkiness.

No one can now be certain of this, but there are good reasons
for believing it. For one thing, vinification was not so certain a
process in those days for it to be likely that white wines could
consistently be produced so limpidly pleasing to the eye as those
of today: it is well within living memory that hock and Moselle
glasses were tinted so as to conceal the lack of limpidity or the
blemishes in the wine. The glasses are still to be found, and in
Germany still occasionally used: green for Moselle, amber for
hock. (Some still have a vestigial tinting of the stems and feet.)

Once the wines of Champagne became established on a national
scale, as distinct from being known largely to the people of the
region, and to distinguished visitors, a great rivalry opened up
between the wine-growers of Champagne and their nearest
neighbours, those of Burgundy.

In so far as the Burgundians did manage to produce reasonably
clear white wines—or to try their best, at any rate—the *cham-*

penois made something of a virtue of their own difficulties in doing so, and seem deliberately to have gone in for the various shades of pink and what I suppose we may loosely call 'off-white'. André Simon quotes a writer of the middle of the seventeenth century as stating that not one of the wines of Champagne was white, but tawny, between white and red, or the colour of honey.

So much for colour. As for taste, one must base one's assumptions partly on what the still champagnes of today are like, partly on what we know to be the kind of wines that Champagne's climate and Champagne's soil would probably always produce.

Champagne is a northerly cool-climate region: its chalky soil is dry and poor. This means, as a similar combination of coolness and poor soil means in Germany and elsewhere, clear, crisp, light wines, high in acidity and low in alcohol. Today, little of the still red wine of Bouzy is made, for the grapes are needed for champagne itself, and little of what *is* made finds its way on to the market; some of it is used to make pink champagne;[4] but one sometimes tastes it at the tables of champagne-making friends, as I have done at Moët et Chândon's Château Saran. It is a light, delicate wine, with something of the taste of burgundy, but with more finesse and less depth, and with nothing like the smell of burgundy, but more of the fresh scent that is so appealing in sparkling champagne. One must assume that Henri IV's still red wine of Ay was a wine of the same sort, though certainly neither so consistent nor so clear.

In the same way, the white or near-white or pinkish still champagne of the time would have tasted much as a bottle of still white champagne would taste now—when one can find it. It would have been dry and delicate, yet fruity in flavour and in fragrance, with a very 'clean' finish. It is noticeable that even nowadays a still champagne is rather deep in colour compared with many of the other white wines of Europe. Mr Patrick Forbes credits it with a 'rich yellow sheen'.

*   *   *

Reims is 165 kilometres from Paris; Beaune is 310. Once the wines of Champagne were known at court, thanks to the interest

[4] See pages 129 *et* seq

of Henri IV, they enjoyed this advantage over the already well-established wines of Burgundy that, other things being equal, they were cheaper by half the cost of transport.

Other things were, in fact, pretty well equal, too, for the red wines of Burgundy and the red wines of Champagne were both made of Pinot grapes—not identical, says André Simon, but sharing 'a certain measure of family likeness', so that 'the wines of Champagne were, like those of Burgundy, red table wines, maybe a little lighter in colour and body but not so very much different'. (I have already shown why I think that only a minority of the wines of Champagne were red. Indeed, André Simon seems to contradict himself here.)

Not that the *champenois* relied on the relative cheapness of their wines compared with those of Burgundy.

Indeed, they spent money on improved methods of vinification, and incurred losses at the vintage by their rigorous selection of only the finest grapes. They were prepared to court the courtiers with wines that cost more than burgundies, but were better because of it, and they had the margin provided by lower transport costs to play with.

By the time that Henri IV's grandson, Louis XIV, had come to the throne, in 1643, the *champenois* were making much not only of their still relatively rare red wines, as being more delicate, more elegant, more suitable to men of fashion, than the red wines of Burgundy, but also of their much more plentiful pink, honey-coloured, and white (or near-white) wines as being unique —wines that could not be matched by any other province of France, and certainly not by Burgundy.

So it was now established among the influential wine-lovers of the time that the wines of Champagne were delicate and were different: the hour had come for the most important development in their history—the hour and the man.

But before we meet the man—a monk, Dom Pérignon—let us first make the acquaintance of a man of fashion.

In 1660, Charles de Marguetel de Saint-Denis, seigneur de Saint-Evremond, was a member of the embassy sent by Louis XIV of France to felicitate Charles II of England on his restoration to the throne. The following year he fell under Louis's displeasure and, recalling the welcome he had received in England, the friends he had made and, no doubt, the gaiety of Charles's court, and the beauty and accessibility of its women, sought refuge there, 'where he was received', André Simon has written, 'with the courtesy due to his rank and the esteem which befitted his merits'.

For Saint-Evremond was a critic as well as a courtier: an essayist and a wit, as much a friend of the playwrights of the Restoration—Etherege, Wycherley, Congreve and the rest—as of the playthings of the court.

His importance in the history of champagne is that this highly cultivated creature—at this time about fifty years old—influential as he was in the worlds of fashion and of letters, was an epicure and a wine-lover: 'the most refined epicurean of his age', according to the Duc d'Aumale.

Charles and many of his courtiers had been in exile in France, and they were very ready to welcome not only Saint-Evremond himself but to listen to his views on eating and drinking. And what Saint-Evremond told them was that his favourite wines, as they were the favourites of the court at Versailles, were those of Champagne, and that the way to drink them was to put down the reds so that they would acquire bottle-age, but to drink the whites very young, the spring after the vintage, when the natural second fermentation gave them a prickle, if not a sparkle.

As early as 1663, Butler refers, in *Hudibras*, to 'brisk Champaign', which certainly suggests sparkle, and Etherege is more positive still, in 1676, when he writes, in *The Man of Mode*:

> To the Mall and the Park
> Where we love till 'tis dark,
> Then sparkling Champaign
> Puts an end to their reign;
> It quickly recovers
> Poor languishing lovers,
> Makes us frolic and gay, and drowns all sorrow;
> But alas, we relapse again on the morrow.

After which, and other contemporary references to 'brisk' champagne, it does not seem fanciful of André Simon to claim that when Farquhar's tavern servant in *Love in a Bottle* (1697) points to the champagne he has brought and says, 'Here, here, Master, how it puns and quibbles in the glass!' it must be the bubbles that he is pointing to.

And André Simon goes on to give overwhelming reasons for stating firmly that it was at this very time, and in England, that the *coupe* or *tazza* was first designed and produced as a champagne glass,[5] and offers considerably more slender grounds for supposing that it might have been at Saint-Evremond's suggestion.

Now there seems to be, if not any very concrete proof, at least reason to suppose that at this time champagne as a reliably sparkling or, at any rate, slightly sparkling or *pétillant* wine was more consistently available and better-known in England than in Paris.

If this was indeed the case, then it was because it was in England, and at just about this time, that new techniques of glassblowing produced heavy, strong glass bottles that could withstand the pressure of sparkling wine inside them—provided they could be stoppered with cork, presumably tied on. And Mr Patrick Forbes has pointed out that as the English 'were a maritime nation in frequent contact with Spain, they had been in possession of cork long before it came to the notice of the landlocked Champenois'. He proves his point by quoting the reference to cork in Rosalind's, 'prithee, take the cork out of thy mouth, that I may drink thy tidings', to Celia in *As You Like It*, written as long as sixty years or more before the time with which we now deal. He might well have added that in *A Winter's Tale*, the Clown describes a ship in a storm as being 'swallowed with yest and froth, as you'd thrust a cork into a hogshead', proving not only an acquaintanceship with cork but also with a 'brisk' wine fermenting in cask.

But if the basic principle of how to preserve the natural sparkle of champagne had thus been first discovered and applied in England, let it not detract from the historical importance of Dom Pérignon, Saint-Evremond's near contemporary,[6] whose discoveries went further and were more fully implemented.

*   *   *

[5] See chapter 9 for a consideration of this and other champagne glasses.
[6] Saint-Evremond, 1613–1703; Dom Pérignon, 1638–1715.

Three miles north of Epernay, looking down upon a great silvery curve of the Marne from its vine-clad slopes, is the pretty village of Hautvillers.

In the abbey church, at the foot of the altar steps, is a black marble slab, the inscription on which records in monkish Latin that beneath it lie the remains of Dom Pierre Pérignon, for forty-seven years the cellarer of that monastery until his death, in 1715, at the age of seventy-seven. There is a modern statue to him in the cloisters, which are now the property of the firm of Moët et Chandon, and scheduled for preservation by the Ministry of Fine Arts as a historic monument, and there is another statue to him in the courtyard of Moët's business premises in the Avenue de Champagne in Epernay.

These honours are not precisely, as is often loosely said and generally supposed, because Dom Pérignon was the 'inventor' of champagne, or 'discovered' the secret of getting the bubbles into it.

As we have seen, champagne tends to sparkle by nature, and the English were referring to champagne as a 'brisk' and a sparkling wine before Dom Pérignon had become the cellarer of the Benedictine monastery of Hautvillers, in 1668, and before there is any similar reference in French literature.

What Dom Pérignon seems to have done—I write 'seems' because although we know some of this, some of it, however well-based, is only assumption—is to have improved the strains of vine and the techniques of making a 'complete' wine by blending the juice of different varieties; to have had cellars dug and *celliers* built (a *cellier* is an above-ground store); discovered how to make both red wine and, more important, really clear 'white' wine from black grapes; and, unaware of developments in England, to have been the first in France to keep the bubble in the bottle by using the new-fangled strong bottles and by tying corks into their necks.

It is a more substantial achievement than it sounds in so bald a summary, for if, as Mr Edward Hyams has written,[7] 'champagne invented itself', nevertheless Dom Pérignon, 'made champagne a manageable wine for commerce. . . . His rational

[7] Edward Hyams, *Dionysus: a Social History of the Wine Vine*, 1965.

approach, his infinite patience in trial-and-error methods, his intellectual integrity, were all typical of the best and rarest kind of scientist. His achievements were to make the judgement of the state of ripeness in the grapes a matter of near certainty; to make blending rational instead of hit-and-miss; and to go some way towards bringing the destructive demon of pressure in the bottles under some sort of control. In short, although handi-capped by want of instruments and forced to rely on his senses instead, he laid down the basic techniques for champagne-making which are still viable.'

Dom Pérignon deserves his statues.

*   *   *

This was the beginning of the modern history of champagne.

It may also be regarded, in a way, as the remotest beginning of the house of Bollinger, for in 1729, only fourteen years after the death of Dom Pérignon, Nicholas Ruinart of Epernay, nephew of a Dom Ruinart who had been Dom Pérignon's contemporary and friend, founded what is thought to be the first firm devoted solely to the making and selling of champagne—certainly still the oldest firm still surviving.[8] As will be seen in chapter 4, the firm that Jacques Bollinger joined in 1822 to learn the champagne trade was that of Muller-Ruinart. Young Antoine Muller, Bollin-ger's boss, had married a Mlle Ruinart, and it is hardly possible to suppose that, living in so small a place, and concerned in the same trade, she was not a member of the same family.

This is not the place to pursue the history of champagne in general, for our concern is with one house in particular. It is enough to record that by the time the name of 'Bollinger' was first put on the label of a champagne bottle, in 1829 (see chapter 4), the golden, sparkling wine had already become as firmly established and as famous at the court of Louis XV, the Well-Beloved and, until he died on the guillotine, of his not so well-beloved grandson. The Pompadour endorsed it as the only wine that leaves a woman still beautiful after drinking it, though a less

---

[8] Moët et Chandon now own a controlling interest in Ruinart, but the firm still enjoys a separate identity.

well-known lady of the court phrased it better with, 'it gives brilliance to the eyes without flushing the face'.

In England, the rich and the high-born, at any rate, enjoyed champagne from the end of the Marlborough wars, in spite of laws against the importation of wine in bottle, and in spite of the heavy taxes against French wines that were not lowered to the level of those on Portuguese wines until Pitt's commercial treaty of 1787.

Neither the Revolution nor war against the Republic and against Napoleon seriously checked the consumption of champagne by England's nobility and gentry, and on 12 April 1814, when Wellington rode into Toulouse at the head of his Peninsular army, to be told that Napoleon had abdicated, it was champagne he called for in which to toast the odious restored Bourbons with three times three.

This was the beginning of a highly significant period in the history of champagne and the champagne trade. 'Still the champagne popped and fizzed,' writes Lady Longford of the days between the taking of Toulouse and the triumphal allied entry into Paris.[9] It popped and fizzed throughout the occupation; it popped and fizzed as the Congress opened in Vienna; it popped and fizzed in Brussels at the Duchess of Richmond's ball; and Waterloo was the best excuse of all for more popping and fizzing. '*Le Congrès ne marche pas, il danse.*' It danced from the summer of 1814 to the late summer of 1815, for months before and for months after Waterloo. And what goes better at a ball than champagne?

Diplomatists and colonels of dragoons from Prussia and from Russia; Swedes and Sicilians and Saxons and Switzers; visiting members of parliament and visiting members of White's; all learned, or were reminded, or reinforced their previously held convictions that bubbles spoke every language, that champagne was the international wine of celebration.

If Dom Pérignon is to be regarded as responsible for making champagne the wine we know today, and Saint-Evremond as having introduced it to the country that is still Champagne's

[9] Elizabeth Longford, *Wellington: the Years of the Sword*, 1969.

best foreign customer, it was the rise and then the fall of Napoleon that made its wider international reputation.

Napoleon himself, we know, was a burgundy man (in a manner of speaking—he used to water his Chambertin) but his officers took their taste for champagne into every capital of Europe and then, in their turn, his conquerors celebrated his downfall in glasses of fizz in the country where it was made, and took a taste for it back home with them. Mr Patrick Forbes dates from the great review of 295,000 Russian troops in 1815 at Mont Aimé, at the southern end of the Côte des Blancs, that passion of Russia's officer caste for champagne that made their country for a hundred years its next biggest customer after Great Britain.[10]

The champagne houses could well have echoed the optimism expressed by Castlereagh to the Tsar at the Congress of Vienna: *'il commence l'âge d'or'*, for the hundred years from then until the outbreak of the First World War was for them a period of progress and prosperity. A reasonably settled Europe—for in spite of 1848, in spite of the Crimea, the Risorgimento, and Sedan, Europe was settled enough for its middle and upper classes not only to survive but to grow richer than ever, and so did those of the booming United States—meant a steady rise in the consumption of every kind of wine, and of champagne in particular.

This was a scientific age, too, which meant that there were solutions now at hand for the champagne-making problems that Dom Pérignon's discoveries, vastly important though they were, had still left unsolved.

A *champenois* named François produced in the 1830s a sugar-measuring apparatus, or *densimètre*, that showed how much natural grape-sugar was left in the wine after the first fermentation. This meant that the champagne-maker knew how much to add at the time of bottling to induce and encourage the second fermentation. Hitherto, it had been a matter of guesswork; too

[10] Though Count Bertrand de Vogüé, in an engaging little booklet, *Madame Clicquot: her Peaceful Conquest of Russia*, published as I prepared this book for the press, points to two shipments of Veuve Clicquot made to Russia in 1814 as giving rise to the great prestige enjoyed there by champagne throughout the next hundred years.

much added sugar for the second fermentation had meant far too many breakages through excessive pressure in the bottle. Many firms were still concentrating on still wines; others played safe, adding little or none, and producing a wine that was not fully sparkling (*mousseux*) but frothy (*crémant*).[11]

The new invention took the speculation out of sparkle: from now on, still champagnes lost their importance, and their production soon became negligible. Fizz came first.

André Simon has said that Madame Bollinger is the best-known of today's numerous 'champagne widows', but widows, by an odd chance, have always been prominent in the champagne trade, and no one—certainly not Madame Bollinger—would begrudge the Veuve Clicquot her place in history. She was a legend in her lifetime, as her name still is, more than a century after her death. The wine that bears that name is still one of the most respected, and 'the widow' was long a pet name for that or, indeed, any other fizz.

Left a widow at the age of twenty-seven, in 1806, she not only saved her father-in-law's champagne-making business from bankruptcy, but by her vigorous business methods and skill in the arts of publicity made world-famous the name of champagne in general and that of her own firm's wine in particular.

All this is certain: what is less certain, but highly probable, and undoubtedly in character, is that she worked out in her own cellars the system, still basically in use today, by which a bottle of champagne is cleared of its sediment after the second fermentation without recourse to decanting, and the consequent danger of loss of effervescence.

It had long been the practice to fill the space left in the bottle by the discharge of the sediment with a liqueur made of the same wine and a proportion of sugar; champagne by nature is austerely and, to most people, unacceptably dry. The amount of sugar in this liqueuring or *dosage* determines the relative sweetness

---

[11] *Crémant* is not to be confused with the vineyard town of Cramant, in the Côte des Blancs. A few firms, but none, I think, of the best-known houses, still make a *crémant* champagne—it comes frothing out of the bottle, but settles down in the glass to a gentle *pétillance*, or prickle, not the pronounced and continuing bubble of the classic champagne.

or dryness of the finished wine, and with the various scientific discoveries and developments of the quarter-century or so that followed the downfall of the first Napoleon this became very precisely determinable. The history of champagne-making and of champagne-drinking for the rest of the century is a history of the change from sweet to dry.

Meanwhile, another Napoleon had become emperor of the French, and the gaieties of the Paris of the Second Empire, to which so many foreigners flocked, meant more international publicity still for the gayest of wines. It was claret that was classified at the Exposition Universelle de Paris in 1855, but it was champagne, surely, that the visitors drank at their little suppers after the Offenbach operettas at the theatre in the Champs Elysées.

That was the world of Napoleon III, the party-giver, the planner of international exhibitions, the husband of a pretty woman, herself surrounded by pretty women. But the other Napoleon III, carbon copy of his uncle, designer of uniforms and rattler of sabres—even he had a share, however indirectly, in the great expansion of the champagne market. There was much fear in Britain of France's military might—look at her victories in Italy! There was much fear of her expansionist policy—she had swallowed Nice and Savoy as the result. There was fear even of her naval strength—for had not the Queen and the Prince Consort been invited to a naval review at Cherbourg to see the new French ironclads? So much so, that the Poet Laureate was urging his countrymen:

'Form, form, Riflemen, form!'

and the two countries were as near war as they had ever been without actually recalling ambassadors.

Cobden, Radical M.P. for Rochdale, persuaded Gladstone, Chancellor of the Exchequer, who needed little persuading, that the way to slacken the tension was to 'get the two nations into debt with each other', and Gladstone sent him off to Paris to negotiate a commercial treaty that brought about virtual free trade between them, and reduced the duty on French wines to no more than the duty on any other.

The provisions of Cobden's commercial treaty were embodied in the Budget of 1860: the duty on French table wines fell to two shillings a dozen (from twelve) and on champagne to five shillings a dozen. Not only that, but the 'single bottle' Act of the following year extended the retail sale of wine, hitherto restricted by law to hotels, public houses and wine-merchants, to any grocer, off-licence or reputable 'refreshment house'. Wine was brought well within the reach of the little man—champagne almost as much so as 'Gladstone claret'.

Within easy enough reach, at any rate, of his cognizance for it not to be thought bizarre for George Leybourne to be singing 'Champagne Charlie' at him in the music-halls of 1869, with its glorification of Moët, and The Great Vance replying with his,

> Clicquot! Clicquot! Drinking other wine is folly,
> Clicquot! Clicquot! That's the drink for me.

A similar audience would not be so familiar today with the great names of champagne.

When the Grossmiths wrote their *Diary of a Nobody* in the late 1880s[12] their Mr Pooter of The Laurels, Brickfield Terrace, Holloway, would send Sarah round to his grocer for a single bottle at a time of *Jackson Frères*, at three-and-sixpence. It may not have been the very best champagne (I fancy that the Grossmiths cannot have known that there was then—and is now—a very reputable Reims firm called Jacquesson et Fils), but it was champagne, and champagne could indeed, in those days, be bought from one's grocer at three-and-sixpence.

André Simon records that those were the days when a bottle of champagne at the Union Club, where it would be a decent brand and have to show a modest profit, cost 5*s*., and only 6*s*. at the Bodega for a bottle to take away. The days, too, when Mr Gladstone, who had brought champagne within the reach of Mr Pooter of The Laurels, would polish off a bottle to himself at dinner.

I think it possible that what Mr Pooter and the customers of the Bodega drank was dry champagne, and more than likely that

---

[12] It was first published in book form in 1892, but had previously appeared as a series in *Punch*.

that was what was drunk by the members of the Union Club and by the Prime Minister.

But it is difficult now to be certain, for the change in Britain from sweet to dry was a pretty slow one. In about 1850, a London wine-merchant shipped the 1846 Perrier-Jouët unliqueured but had to return it because it did not please his customers. But he persevered, and it is clear that by the end of that decade and the beginning of the next, sophisticated Englishmen drank their champagne dry. The cartoonists of *Punch* do not lead, they reflect, middle-class English taste, and as early as 12 April 1862 we have a schoolboy at a John Leech dinner-party telling his uncle that the champagne is 'H'm—awfully sweet! Very good sort for ladies—but I've arrived at a time of life, when I confess I like my wine *dry!*'

All the same, Professor Saintsbury (who quoted the once celebrated description, 'A man who likes [or "who would say he likes"] dry champagne') wrote that the change from sweet to dry was not finally accomplished when he was making the first entries in his cellar-book, in 1884.

In France, the change came much later: champagne was still a sweet dessert wine there in the 1890s, and then the change came pretty abruptly at about the turn of the century. This was confirmed for me by a chance discovery a few years ago in an Edinburgh bookshop.

Side by side, on a shelf devoted to books about eating and drinking, I found the first edition and the third of *The Gourmet's Guide to Europe*: the one published in 1903 and described as being, 'by Lieut-Col Newnham-Davis and Algernon Bastard, edited by the former'; the other published in 1911, with no reference on the title-page to Mr Bastard, but a note in the preface recording with much regret his death.

I had always wanted a copy of what, in its modest way, is a pioneer work, and I suppose a serious bibliophile would have been satisfied with the first edition. Finding, though, that the one copy cost only three shillings, and the other no more than four, I decided to hang the expense and take the two. My excuse to myself for my extravagance was that there might be illuminating differences between the gastronomic Europe of 1903 and that of 1911.

Even without any very scholarly collation of the two editions, I was soon justified. I found the colonel observing in 1903 that, 'as to the champagnes found abroad, unless they are specially made for the English market, they must not be judged from an English standpoint, being as a rule far too sweet for our taste'. And he went on to recall staying at Reims (I suppose a year or so earlier), 'for some shooting owned by a syndicate of some of the larger champagne shippers. We met for *déjeuner* at their Châlet de Chasse or club-house, each gentleman bringing his own wine. The result was that one saw from ten to a dozen different famous brands of champagne on the table.

'My host asked me which sort I would prefer. "*Du vin Brut*, if you have any," I replied. "*Ah! Vous buvez de ce poison-là?*" exclaimed he, smiling. So they evidently did not agree with our taste for dry wine.'

Nowadays, of course, the taste of French champagne-shippers —of any serious French drinker of champagne, indeed—is at least as austere as that of those good customers, the English, and I wondered when the change took place. To my delight, I found that the whole anecdote had been omitted from the 1911 edition and not, presumably, simply on grounds of space, for the third edition is twice as long as the first, and it was so good a story that I think the author would only have cut it out because it had become dated.

Edward VII, as Prince of Wales and as King, was a heavy smoker and a gross eater, but he drank sparingly. He preferred champagne to claret or burgundy, and this, too, gave the wine an especial cachet. Indeed, he had given an early start to the change from a taste for sweet to a taste for dry champagne through the liking he showed for the 'Very Dry' Ayala 1865 when he re-visited his old Oxford club, the Bullingdon, round about 1870. And he is held to be responsible, if only indirectly, for a nick-name that clung to champagne for more than half a century. It came to be called 'the boy' by Edwardian and late-Victorian heavy swells after a shooting-party—so it is said—at which the corpulent, champagne-loving Prince of Wales was present. A lad was responsible for the wheelbarrow of champagne, packed in ice. It was a hot day, and the number of times the thirsty prince bellowed 'Boy!' led to a transference of epithet from the cup-bearer to the cup—especially by those who wished to make it known that they had been shooting that day with the heir to the throne. And it persisted beyond their generation: as recently as the 1930s a Salisbury hotel-keeper I knew, who had been a friend of Harry Preston's and C. B. Cochran's, used to model his way of life on that of such *bon vivants*, even to the extent of a mid-morning imperial pint of fizz—and even to the extent of calling it, 'a bottle of the Boy'.

There are those who facetiously spell and pronounce it 'the Bhoy', and those, too, who hold that the nickname applies not to champagne in general but to Bollinger in particular, just as 'a bottle of the widow' would specifically indicate a bottle of Veuve Clicquot. It would be agreeable both to the author and to the subject of this book if it could be proved to be so, but I am bound to admit that I had always thought 'the Boy' a generic term for a bottle of any brand until 1969, when Mr Cunison Deans Rankin, whose family has grown and shipped cork for generations, and has always therefore known the wine trade well, assured me that 'the Bhoy' was Bollinger.

'If memory serves', he wrote, 'both my dear old father and my late Uncle John, who were at their prime at the turn of the century, made a habit, when entertaining ladies in the West End to supper after the theatre, to offer them two alternatives, the Widow or the Bhoy, and I have always understood that this was the general practice of young men about town in those late Victorian and early Edwardian days.'

It may have been so, but did no one ever offer any other champagne but Clicquot or Bollinger?

However that may be, Mr Rankin went on to tell me not only that he too, like my Salisbury acquaintance, was still referring to 'the Bhoy' in the 1930s, but that it was Bollinger he meant: he and a wine-trade friend used to crack a bottle whenever either of them broke eighty on their annual Scottish golfing holiday.

*   *   *

By that time, of course, champagne had been the wine of celebration for a couple of hundred years, since long before nineteenth holes were first played by holidaying Englishmen. I cannot discover when it was first used to launch ships—a sad waste of champagne, it seems to a consumer, though a source of profit and of publicity to the trade—but the late William Younger[13] found what might well be the first recorded instance of its being drunk out of a lady's slipper in *The Connoisseur* of 6 June 1754. The lady was no better than she should be: I hope the wine was.

Once the wine had come to be made fully sparkling, the very appearance of the bottle became festive. The wire muzzle is necessary to hold on the cork, but it is unsightly—all the more so when it has rusted in the cellar. So there has to be a foil cover, and it may as well be gold or silver, or some such gay material. There has to be ceremony in the uncorking, or else the cork will pop—and either the ceremony or the pop disposes one to jollity.

Then the expense. Champagne cannot be cheap: there are so many processes requiring skilled labour; the bottles must be especially strong, the corks particularly stout; the very muzzling and dressing-up in foil we have mentioned is expensive, both in material and in time. The fact that a dish or a wine is expensive makes it something one puts aside for a celebration; and what one puts aside for a celebration tends to attract the tax-gatherer— in every champagne-drinking country in the world, including the one in which it is made, champagne is taxed more heavily than still wine—in the United Kingdom, 19p a bottle more than a still wine imported in cask and bottled here—which makes it more expensive still, and still more, therefore, a wine for special occasions.

But the wine itself is gay, and the cause of gaiety in those who drink it. Not only do the very bubbles laugh at one: they carry the alcohol into the bloodstream more quickly than happens with a still wine—one gets an immediate 'lift' or 'kick' from champagne but, so long as it is not a heavily sugared wine, there is little to pay for it next day in the form of a hangover. Champagne is light in texture, body and taste (though its alcohol

[13] William Younger, *Gods, Men and Wine*, 1966.

content is usually a little higher than that of a claret) so that it is easy both on the head and the stomach.

It is the clean finish, fresh in the mouth, that makes champagne such a good apéritif: it is the immediate tonic effect of the quickly released alcohol that makes it such a good pick-me-up and so good at a party. John Jorrocks said, nearly a century and a half ago, 'it gives one werry gentlemanly ideas'. Or as Mr Alan Brien put it, only the other day, 'the sensation of being given a physical lift, like water wings'.

*   *   *

Bollinger was one of the first houses to ship a 'Very Dry' to England—it certainly shipped, like Ayala, a 'Very Dry' 1865, and the firm can regard itself as having been one of the leaders of the revolution in English taste that M. Simon places in the 1870s. For the change came slowly, as we have seen from Professor Saintsbury's *Notes on a Cellar-Book* where he recorded that 'the head of the great house of Roederer was, even later [than 1884], said to have declared that as long as *he* lived there should be no bowing to the dry Baal in his cellars; and, at any rate in the country, Clicquot was more often still sweet—not to the "Russe" extent, which was only good for savages or children, but yet not dry.' And he confesses that in 1878 when he told his pawky Scottish Pall Mall wine-merchant that he did not share the prevailing mania for Pommery (another of the pioneers of 'Very Dry' on the English market) 'he looked at me approvingly and said, "I'd nearly as soon have a bra-a-andy and sod-d-a!"'

It was Saintsbury's view that, 'if you only keep sufficient wine-flavour in dry wines (they are apt to lose it) nobody of catholic taste would desire their abolition, though one may regret the moderately rich and full-flavoured variety as an alternative'.

Saintsbury, who was a boorish reactionary bully, did not know all that much about wine, either. Most good champagne-makers could tell him—Bollinger certainly would—that even 'moderately rich' champagnes have obscured their 'wine-flavour' with sugar, and that the drier a really well-made skilfully-blended champagne, the more truly the real flavour of the wine shows itself. Nor is it 'apt to lose' this flavour.

Bollinger's present very dry, very full-flavoured, style has been the speciality of the house for a very long time—perhaps since the deed of partnership between the first Jacques Bollinger and his son Joseph, in the 1860s, reserving to the father the making of the *cuvée*, or blend.

Documentary evidence is sparse, but M. Christian Bizot, Madame Bollinger's nephew and the firm's sales director, believes that not only was the house of Bollinger, 'one of the very first to sell Very Dry wines to your country'—this we know from other sources—but also as early with very dry wine in other markets; 'I believe also that there was no time lag between English and French markets. The only way I can prove this is by the fact that our labels of the second half of the nineteenth century bear the words Very Dry for the English market and Brut for other markets.' (The difference in language is maintained to this day on the Special Cuvée, which is to say the non-vintage labels: 'Very Dry' for the British market, 'Brut' elsewhere. But it is amusing to observe that Bollinger would appear to expect English customers for vintage Bollinger, if not for the non-vintage, to know their French—it is 'Brut' on the vintage labels for all markets.)

If M. Bizot is right, then Bollinger were well ahead of fashion in France where, as Colonel Newnham-Davis's anecdote shows, most champagne-makers themselves were still drinking sweet champagne at the very end of the century. Bollinger must have had considerable confidence in their own blend, and been very sure that a dry wine, so long as it was so well made from such good grapes that it kept what Saintsbury called 'wine-flavour', would eventually prove the true wine-lover's choice. And it is perhaps significant that it was at this period, in 1884, that Joseph Bollinger, Madame Bollinger's grandfather-in-law, was granted a royal warrant as supplier of champagne to Queen Victoria: the firm has held the royal appointment to every British monarch since.

There are no presidential appointments in the United States as there are royal appointments here, but Bollinger and Julius Wile Sons and Co., Inc., who have been their agents there ever since repeal, must take an amused pride in a tribute of quite another sort, though at least as sincerely meant. When the vastly rich

James McMillan Gibson died at Palm Beach in 1966[14] his will revealed that 'I want to be remembered as a "champagne boy"; I want to be buried with a bottle of champagne at my head and another bottle at my feet.' True to his testamentary wishes, a blue-grey model, more than three feet high, of a nebuchadnezzar of Bollinger, so inscribed, was placed at either end of his grave, where they remained until the cars of the curious had worn a track through the cemetery grass, to the annoyance of the relatives of others who lay there, and authority required their removal. They now stand in the widow's garden, silent testimony to a husband's extra-marital love affair.

[14] James McMillan Gibson was fifty-six when he died. He had houses in Palm Beach, on the Maine coast, and in Europe. He sold his house in Washington, D.C., to the then Mrs John Kennedy. He was descended on both sides of his family from United States senators and had himself been on the staff of Edward Stettinius, Secretary of State at the time of the setting up of the United Nations Organization.

3. Lords and Commons

THE Route du Champagne offers three itineraries, all marked by signs bearing a bunch of white grapes, a vine-leaf, and the white plume that symbolizes, says the Comité, the *panache* of the wine and of the way it is drunk. Each offers a delightful drive of an hour or so, whether over the downs, along the river or through the woods, but always within sight of vineyards, or with the promise of vineyards round the next corner.

Many of these are marked with small boundary stones bearing the names of the famous houses that own them. Others belong to small growers who sell to these same great houses, for none owns enough vineyards to provide all the grapes it needs. Other growers sell to champagne-making houses, equally famous, that own no vineyards at all. And still others to growers who do not sell their grapes at all, but use it to make their own single-vineyard champagne.

There are said to be 144 champagne firms making the traditional blended wine, each with their own brand name or names; and 15,000 vineyard owners, of which number 3,000 are *manipulants*, making their own wine from their own vineyards.

In Britain we tend to call the big champagne firms 'shippers', though this can be confusing, as we use the same word for those firms on our own side of the Channel that import wines. These in their turn should not be confused with single-brand agents, such as the London firm of Mentzendorff, who act only for Bollinger.

Bollinger call themselves *négociants*, even though this implies that they are middlemen, which of course they are not, because although they are makers of champagne they dislike the word *fabriquant* which, says M. Christian Bizot, suggests a button-maker or some such. I think it best to refer to the big makers of the wine as champagne 'firms' or champagne 'houses'.

Some of the 144 are specialists in B.O.B.—'buyer's own brand' —champagnes, bought by retail wine-merchants, the wine departments of department stores, and so on, to carry their own labels and their own name, and be sold rather more cheaply than the well-known *marques*. Thus, the Army and Navy Stores has its 'Achille Morat', Justerini and Brooks their 'Sarcey', and my own Directors' Wine Club, along with other subsidiaries of International Distillers and Vintners, our 'Lambert', of which we are not at all ashamed—it is a sound wine, bought from a sound firm—though these B.O.B. wines are never in the same class as the wines that the leading houses sell under their own names. It is not at all unusual for the same B.O.B. wine to be sold under half a dozen different names by half a dozen different retail firms: but usually the more pretentious the name, the more dubious the bottle.

Wines made by *manipulants* can be bought by the roadside, as motorists in England buy eggs or strawberries. Some find their way into the village shop or the local restaurant. Some that are made on a big enough scale may also become B.O.B. brands. They are always much cheaper than the well-known brands (about 14.50 francs by the roadside, 16 francs at a village grocer —£1.10, say, and £1.25 respectively, whereas a respectable *grande marque* in a decent retail shop would cost more than a couple of pounds—Bollinger or Krug more still). As is to be expected, they vary enormously, too, in quality. As André Simon has pointed out,[1] (using the word vigneron where *manipulant* would be rather more precise):

[1] André Simon, *The History of Champagne*, 1962.

The wines sold by shippers and vignerons are by no means the same, although they are all made within the legal limits of the *délimitation* and are all equally entitled to the name of Champagne. They differ basically on account of the difficulty for the vignerons of making Champagne in the traditional manner which gave Dom Pérignon's wines their superiority over all others: that is, the happy blending of wines made from grapes in different Champagne vineyards. In many cases, this is impossible for them. Most vignerons have no choice but to sell the Champagne made from the grapes of their own vineyards. . . .

Champagne from the grapes of one Champagne village can indeed be very good, but Champagne made from a blend of black and white Pinots,[2] some from the Montagne de Reims vineyards, some from the Valley of the Marne, and some from the Côte des Blancs, is a much better wine, more balanced, more complete and more lasting, not merely keeping alive for a greater number of years, but gaining power as well as charm with age. The 'single' Champagne of most vignerons is not made to last: it is made to be drunk as soon as possible, when its freshness and lower cost are very real assets . . . a cheaper Champagne than that which bears the famous name of one of the *Grandes Marques*.

There is no such precise definition of the *grandes marques* champagnes as there is of the *crus classés* of Bordeaux.

There is a Syndicat de Grandes Marques in Champagne that adds to its number by election and is pretty particular about whom it elects: Mercier, elected at the end of 1964, took a long time to be accepted, and met some pretty stout opposition, in spite of being then one of the biggest firms in the trade. (It has now merged with the biggest, Moët et Chandon, to form a giant indeed, though each *marque* retains its separate identity.)

There are some firms that seem to decide for themselves that they are *grandes marques*, and no one to say them nay.

But there are twelve firms the qualifications of which are

[2] *Sic:* it is now recognized that the white champagne grape, the Chardonnay, sometimes called the Pinot Chardonnay, is not a Pinot at all.

unassailable: the twelve champagne houses that in 1956, regarding themselves then as the leading firms shipping to Britain under their own labels—leading not necessarily in quantity, though their shipments had to be sizeable—established the Champagne Academy. These twelve, without at all disparaging other notable firms, regard themselves as the *grandes marques*.

Every year, their British agents each select a young member of the wine or the catering trade (always from a firm other than their own) to undergo a fortnight's course in Champagne, each staying at one of the principal's houses, seeing the vintage and the cellar-work, and visiting bottle and cork factories. There is an examination that takes some passing, and a diploma that is worth having.

A very few—very few indeed—of the most eminent firms are outside the scheme, and there are some outside that are bigger than some that are inside, but in any debate about which are the *grandes marques*, it is well to know that the twelve that founded the Champagne Academy are, in alphabetical order:

> Bollinger
> Charles Heidsieck
> Heidsieck Dry Monopole
> Krug
> Lanson
> Moët et Chandon
> Mumm
> Perrier-Jouët
> Pol Roger
> Pommery
> Roederer
> Veuve Clicquot.[3]

As the biggest market for champagne outside France itself, Britain owes these twelve very distinguished firms a debt of

[3] It is fair to say that there may be one or two good firms that could never reach any *grande marque* list as being too small, and that others may well make very good wine indeed but sell most of it in France, or some country other than Britain, and be little-known here. That very sound Ay neighbour of Bollinger, the old-established Deutz and Geldermann, is an example; Henriot another.

gratitude not only for the quality of their wines but for the very substantial contribution they make to the range of knowledge of members of the British wine trade.

But the champagne trade as a whole owes them an even greater debt: for these twelve Champagne Academy houses were the same twelve that took action in the British courts on behalf of the trade as a whole against the British Costa Brava Wine Company in what became known as 'The Spanish Champagne Case'. The Costa Brava Wine Company was selling, and widely publicizing, a Spanish sparkling wine, that was not only not champagne but not even made by the champagne process (or entitled to be called champagne in Spain), as 'Spanish champagne'.

The champagne interests in general, supported by the British Association of Champagne Shippers and by the powerful body (Institut National des Appellations d'Origine des Vins et Eaux-de-vie—I.N.A.O.) responsible under French law for the protection of wine names, authorized these twelve distinguished houses to take legal action on behalf of the trade as a whole.

So 'Bollinger and Others'—in the documents in the case Bollinger acquired a fortuitous prominence by the accident of alphabetical order—brought a criminal prosecution under the Merchandise Marks Act. An Old Bailey jury, the day before Christmas 1958, found the Costa Brava Company not guilty of applying a false or misleading description to the wine they shipped, and the champagne interests had to pay the defendants' costs.

This, to use the words of Mr Robert Keeling, of the firm of Monier, Williams and Keeling, the solicitors who acted for them, made the champagne interests fear that, 'if nothing was done to repair the damage of the Old Bailey verdict, there might be an avalanche of spurious Champagnes on sale in England from wine-producing countries all over the world, and that Champagne might quickly become only a synonym for "sparkling wine" without any geographical significance at all. So again they went back to the law to see if a High Court judge would give them the remedy under the general common law of England which a jury failed to give them under the criminal law.' He continued:

The new action needed courage. Having chosen what appeared to have been the easier path via the Old Bailey and having failed to break through, the Champagne interests were now attempting the more ambitious step of obtaining an injunction to restrain the sale of 'Spanish Champagne' on the ground that this was 'passing off' as Champagne a wine which was not Champagne. . . .[4]

Courage was rewarded on 16 December 1960, when Mr Justice (now Lord Justice) Danckwerts granted 'Bollinger and Others' their injunction restraining the Costa Brava Wine Company from selling Perelada under any name that included the word 'champagne', and gave them forty-eight hours to change their labels.

Quite the most spirited account of the two cases was written by the late Ernest Atkinson,[5] who summed it up:

Altogether it took two years and two courts of law to achieve this costly but valuable victory for the champagne interests. Since the costs of the final action fell on the defence that was not too bad for the plaintiffs. The happy consumer, true beneficiary of all this, has the advantage now of knowing that if a bottle bearing the noun 'champagne' on its label does not contain champagne from Champagne its purveyors, following the decision now established, would be guilty of passing off.

Of course, 'Bollinger and Others' were indemnified as to their costs in the first action by the trade as a whole, which underwrote what might have been desperately heavy expenses in the second but, all the same, the twelve Champagne Academy houses I have listed were chosen by their competitors to carry the flag of Champagne into two heavily-fought battles, and they deserve well of the trade.

* * *

Now amongst these twelve *grandes marques* wines and, at most,

[4] Robert Keeling, 'The "Spanish Champagne" Case'; chapter 17 in André Simon, *The History of Champagne*, London, 1962.
[5] 'Two Cases of Champagne' in *Compleat Imbiber*, 4, London, 1961.

half a dozen others, it is hard to say that one is better than another. Choosing between them is a matter of personal taste, because they do not on the whole vary so much in quality as in style. Some are drier, some a little less dry; some are light and 'crisp'; some fuller-bodied.

So everyone has his favourite champagne: Winston Churchill was devoted throughout a long lifetime to Pol Roger, and André Simon, who lived even longer, shouldered his burden of years with a beaming smile and bottles of Pommery.

I have written that it is hard to say that any one of the dozen and a half or so leading brands is better than any other. Some would say that it is hard, but not impossible. Of course, standards vary—one house may decide to concentrate more than it had been doing on quantity, less on quality; another may go the other way. Some houses continue happily to combine a regard for both.

But I do not think there has been any change in the policy of any of the five firms that Mr Hugh Johnson named in 1966:[6]

> Some houses raise their standards and some lower them as time goes on. No rating of these houses [he had named a couple of dozen leading champagne firms] has any permanent value. It is none the less worth mentioning that if an *hors concours* class were to be made at present, the names which are likely to appear in it are among the following: Bollinger, Krug, Pol Roger, Louis Roederer, Veuve Clicquot.

And I am told by Sir Geoffrey Macnab, secretary of the Government Hospitality Fund from 1957 to 1968, that since the war and until now, after his own time, these same five are the only houses whose vintage champagnes have been bought by the Fund, which has been responsible in that time for the wines served at the luncheons, receptions and dinners given by seven heads of government—Attlee, Churchill, Sir Anthony Eden, Mr Macmillan, Sir Alec Douglas-Home, Mr Wilson and, now, Mr Heath—and their ministers. (At very large receptions, where non-vintage champagne has been served, Perrier-Jouët has been

[6] Hugh Johnson, *Wine*, London, 1966.

added to the list.) The Fund's wines are chosen by a committee composed of a very senior civil servant or former civil servant and similarly eminent wine-shippers.

These five outstanding wines do not vary so widely between themselves in style as do the whole dozen of the Champagne Academy houses, but I should say—and this is a very tentative personal view—that Bollinger is the fullest-flavoured of the five, followed by Veuve Clicquot, and then Pol Roger, Krug and Roederer, in that order, though none is a very 'light' wine. I am even more sure that Bollinger is the driest than I am that it is the fullest, followed closely by Krug, and then Pol Roger, Roederer and Veuve Clicquot in descending order of dryness, though none is at all the slightest bit sweet. They are all uncommonly good wines, and choice between them would be largely subjective.

As will be seen, therefore, Bollinger is particularly dry, and very full in flavour—and I present this as an objective description of an individual champagne's style, not as a disparagement of wines that are lighter in body and a hint less dry, such as many amateurs of good champagne may well, and some do, prefer.

The dryness is controlled by the liqueuring, as will be seen in chapter 6, and the fullness comes, not from Bollinger's using more black grapes in its blend than other houses—I imagine that its proportions of black and white are much the same as those of any other *grande marque*—but from the quality of the black grapes and the particular area (and the particular vineyards within that area) that they come from.

It is to be remembered that Ay is not only the home of Bollinger but also that it sets the Bollinger style. The Ay vineyards face south across the Marne, and the grapes ripen early, so that they are richer and more flavoury at vintage time than others of the same variety from less favoured sites.

Finally, and also because of the maturity of high-quality grapes, Bollinger is as full in fragrance as in flavour: Colonel Andrew Graham has written of it in *The Times* that, 'vintage Bollinger (or can it be just my imagination?) has a bouquet like the day when spring first comes to Paris'.

4. A Champagne Family

Because of its place on the map, and because of the lie of the land, wide open to its neighbours, Champagne has always been a meeting-place of peoples, whether of peoples meeting in battle, or of peoples meeting to do business.

The vast cemeteries of two world wars bear witness to the battles—or to the most recent of them, for this is to say nothing of earlier campaigns and campaigners, from Attila the Hun to the men who marched Napoleon into abdication in 1814. That was the first Napoleon; as for the other—Sedan is a town of Champagne.

It is impossible to reach the great vineyards of the region from any direction without passing British or American, French or German or Italian cemeteries of our own century. There is even a French memorial, at Mondement, by the marshes of Saint-Gond, the southernmost point reached by the German armies in the First World War, on which the French inscription is in pseudo-Arabic script, in honour of the Moroccan troops who stood there, and died there, in September 1914; and a pretty little onion-domed chapel at a Russian cemetery, lost in the lonely meadows that lie south of the road from Ste Menehould to Reims, where the bones of Cossacks have lain since 1916.

And as for Champagne, the great vineyard that for generations past has attracted the adventurous and the ambitious from outside France to blend and to ship the wines grown by its *vignerons*, one need only look at the names of so many of the champagne houses: Krug, Roederer, Mumm, the Heidsiecks, Giesler, Deutz and Geldermann. There are pretty well as many Dutch and German names as there are French.

Bollinger, too, is a German name, but although all the present directors of what is still a private family firm are in one way or another related, only one of them has Bollinger blood—and of that only a trace, from a great-grandfather: at most, I suppose, this makes him one-eighth German (I can never work out these fractional descents). At any rate, he is very much a Frenchman, and a *champenois* at that.

Indeed, all are French and thoroughly so, of course, but the others have Scottish blood too (or, in one case, with a wife of the same Scottish blood). French and Scottish blood, a German name, and yet completely French: nothing could be more *champenois*.

*   *   *

Although, by his own wish, his name did not appear in its books or on its labels, Athanase-Louis-Emmanuel de Villermont—later Admiral Comte de Villermont—was the true founder of the firm of Bollinger, and even to some extent the founder of its fortunes, and there are Bollinger vines rooted to this day in what were once his vineyards, just as there is de Villermont blood in the veins of one of the firm's directors.

It is interesting to record, in the context of what has already been written about Champagne as a meeting-place of peoples, that the house of Hennequin, later to be known as 'de Villermont', is supposed to be of Flemish origin. Indeed, the similarity between 'Hennequin' and 'Heineken' is too marked to pass unnoticed. But the family was firmly established near Troyes, on the upper reaches of the Seine, capital of the county of Champagne, as early as the beginning of the fourteenth century, and

III   The black grape (above) that
gives champagne its body, the
Pinot Noir; and the white
grape, the Chardonnay, that
gives the wine its finesse.

Amiral Comte de Villermont, 1762–1840

Jacques-Joseph-Placide Bollinger, 1803–1884

Jacques Bollinger, 1894–1941

Elisabeth Bollinger, 1899–

IV

in 1359 its then head was ennobled by King John the Good of France for his services in the Hundred Years' War against the English.

By the end of the following century, the family had moved from the neighbourhood of Troyes, which was probably then, as it is now, sausage and ham and cheese country, northwards into the wine-growing middle part of Champagne, near Chalons, on the Marne. They became lords of Villermont, and of much else, linked themselves by marriage with the noblest families of the county and, by the time that Athanase-Louis-Emmanuel was born, in 1763, were owners of vineyards in what were already known to be the best vine-bearing areas of the region—in Ay, Bouzy, Cuis and Verzenay.

But Athanase-Louis-Emmanuel was a younger son, and he was brought up to be, not a landowner, but a professional naval officer. A cadet at fifteen, he was barely seventeen before he was a sub-lieutenant in American waters, in even greater danger from the fevers that ravaged the French line-of-battle ships that were then supporting Washington's and Lafayette's land forces than from the guns of the British squadrons.[1] At eighteen, he was an officer in the fleet with which Admiral de Grasse beat the British in the mouth of Chesapeake Bay—the beginning of the end of the American War of Independence.

By the time that a French had followed an American revolution, de Villermont was twenty-six and a seasoned fighting sailor. He remained a King's man, too, so that when the 'armies of the princes' massed on the frontiers of France to face the ragged columns of the young republic, the naval officer was with them as an officer of artillery, though he soon went back to sea— gladly, perhaps—as a captain in the Imperial Russian Navy, a move which was to prove of unexpected benefit more than twenty years later, when de Villermont was back on his estates at Ay, and the invading Russian armies of 1814, pursuing

---

[1] There is a vivid account in G. O. Trevelyan, *George III and Charles Fox*, volume I, chapter VI, of the condition of the French royal navy at precisely this time, mentioning the ships of the Comte de Guichen, one of the lieutenants-general of the fleet, in whose squadron young de Villermont was serving.

Napoleon to Paris, looked very likely to sack the little town. De Villermont had known the officer commanding the Russian troops in his years as an *emigré*, and Ay was spared.

For by this time de Villermont had made his peace with the new régime, though he was still royalist enough to decline the naval appointment that Napoleon offered him, and that his skill, experience and steadfastness in battle merited. But his share of the family's estates had remained intact, much of the land under vines.

When the Bourbons were restored, he was still in his prime, and was soon appointed governor of the Royal Naval College at Angoulême, and promoted rear-admiral. But he did not, so far as I can discover, ever fly his flag at sea: although his estates were intact, his fortunes needed repair, and he turned to his vineyards for the mending material.

No doubt, like other French noblemen and gentlefolk, the de Villermonts had for many generations past made a little money— some of them had probably made a lot—by selling to their friends and relatives and neighbours such wine as they did not need for their own tables.

De Villermont wasted no time in resuming the eighteenth-century practice. No sooner had the Treaty of Fontainebleau been signed, and Napoleon on his way to Elba, than we find him, in 1814, shipping bottles of still and of sparkling (*crémant*)[2] wine to Jersey and to Guernsey—three dozen of the 1812 still wine and three of the 1806 *crémant* to John Doyle, governor of Jersey; six dozen of the 1811 *crémant* to Robert Cowan and Co., of Guernsey, and four dozen of the 1812 still champagne to Madame Dougald of the same island—all, whether still or sparkling, 1806, 1811 or 1812, at five shillings a bottle.

This suggests quite a good business in the de Villermont wines, but in spite of this, and in spite of the example set by the noble family of Brulart at Sillery, it was not yet the accepted thing for a family such as that of de Villermont, now an admiral and a count, to go whole-heartedly into trade—not even into the wine trade—or even to allow its name to appear on a bottle-label.

[2] For the difference in degree of sparkle between '*crémant*' and '*mousseux*' see p. 35, footnote.

And this is where the Bollingers come in.

*   *   *

Joseph-Jacob-Placide Bollinger (later known as Jacques-Joseph-Placide Bollinger), was born in what was then the independent kingdom of Württemberg in 1803, the son of a senior legal official at the royal court and of his wife, daughter of the minor nobility. So Jacques Bollinger was of good birth, too, but he did not disdain to turn his hand to trade.

Like de Villermont, he was a younger son but, unlike de Villermont, he had no vineyards of his own. He had his way to make, and he proposed to make it by means of other people's vineyards.

In those early decades of the nineteenth century there was something of a high road from Germany and Holland to Champagne being beaten out by the feet of ambitious young men who could sense that there was money to be made in a world newly at peace and anxious to trade, by selling the wine of luxury and good living to those who had learned to love it in occupied Paris, or at the Congress of Vienna. In 1822, at the age of nineteen, that is what Joseph-Jacob-Placide Bollinger proposed to do.

The firm that young Bollinger joined in order to learn his trade—which was that of selling, not of making, wine—had only just been established. Antoine Muller, another German, born in Bavaria, having been for a dozen years *chef de cave* to Madame Clicquot, the famous 'widow', had recently married a Mlle Ruinart. Whether or not she was a member of the family, she bore the name of what is now the oldest existing champagne firm and even in those days was of time-honoured distinction. He set up a champagne-making firm of his own, linking her name with his, and set about selling his wines with uncommon vigour, including advertisements in the Russian press[3], and the recruiting of salesmen to cover other promising foreign markets.

Young Bollinger was an obvious choice to sell in Germany

[3] Mr Patrick Forbes records an interesting exchange in the Russian newspapers between the new firm of Muller-Ruinart and Mme Clicquot, who announced that Muller's resignation 'has in no way affected the limpidity of my wine'.

a champagne made by a fellow-German: he became Muller-Ruinart's representative in what were still the independent kingdoms of Bavaria, Württemberg, Saxony and Hanover, as well as in the Netherlands.

Exactly how Jacques Bollinger fell in with de Villermont is not recorded, but more in those days even than now the champagne trade must have been a closely-knit community, where everyone knew everyone else. So that when the older man saw that there was a bigger future in his wines than selling even three and four and six dozen a time to the Channel Islands, and set up a private limited company in 1829 to exploit them, here was a keen young man, with seven years' experience, to help him to realize it.

So the active partners in the new company were Jacques Bollinger, still in his twenties, and a French colleague of his from Muller-Ruinart, only five years older: Paul Renaudin. It was understood and agreed that de Villermont's name was not to appear on the new company's labels.

Paul Renaudin resigned his partnership within a mere couple of years, but although his name is no longer included in the title of the company, the firm's labels bear the style 'Renaudin, Bollinger and Co.' to this day—though nobody has ever called the wine anything but 'Bollinger'.

Bollinger must have been quite a character. He was not of the same nationality as de Villermont nor, though of gentle birth, quite of the same social class. He was prepared to be a salesman and to see his name on bottles and cases, where de Villermont was not. Nevertheless, he was not long in clinching socially what must have been his commercial success. In 1837, thirty-four years old, already a partner of some eight years' standing, he married Louise-Charlotte, only just twenty, daughter of Amiral Comte de Villermont by his second marriage, to the comtesse de Brettes. So the bride was a French noblewoman on both sides of her family and, from the next generation, the Bollingers were also, by blood, Frenchmen of noble descent. (Bollinger himself was naturalized in 1854, and in the documents of the time is often referred to as 'Bollinger de Villermont'.)

*   *   *

So much, then, for the French blood and for the German name. Let us seek now the Scottish strain.

Almost a century and a half before the formation of Renaudin, Bollinger and Co., on 9 April 1694, two young men had met in the misty forenoon at Bloomsbury Square, in London, to debate with their swords a difference that may or may not have been over a lady.

They were both in their twenties; both young men of fashion. So much so, that each was nicknamed 'Beau'. The one who was to be left on the duelling-ground was 'Beau Wilson', whose enigmatic way of life is touched upon, but not explained, in Evelyn's *Diary*.[4]

The other, sometimes styled 'Beau', sometimes 'Jessamy John', was John Law of Lauriston, son of an Edinburgh goldsmith-banker, heir to Lauriston Castle, near Edinburgh (now a museum), and already, at twenty-three, 'nicely expert in all manner of debaucheries'.

According to the evidence of an eye-witness who appeared at the subsequent trial, Law made, 'but one pass by which Mr Wilson received a mortal wound in the upper part of the stomach of the depth of two inches, of which he instantly died'.

Before he could get away, Law was arrested, and taken to Newgate. He was sentenced to death, and reprieved; but Beau Wilson's brother lodged an 'appeal of murder'—a form of civil legal process, already antiquated even in those days, which the widow or male heir of the deceased victim of violence could bring after the killer had been found guilty but reprieved or pardoned.

Law did not wait for a second verdict, for if it went against him this time there could be no further reprieve.

[4] And those who enjoy pursuing fact into fiction should know that Sir Gavin Walpole-Wilson of Hinton Hoo, the diplomatist in Anthony Powell's 'Music of Time' series of novels who 'had left the Foreign Office under a cloud' (and whose wife believed that, 'with a different collection of guests in the house things might take a turn for the better'), claimed in *A Buyer's Market* that, 'I expect you have heard of Beau Wilson, a young gentleman who spent a lot of money in the reign of William and Mary, and was killed in a duel. I have reason to suppose he was one of our lot.'

Only escape.[5]

Law was lodged in the King's Bench Prison to await the hearing of the second action.

He had rich and powerful friends, which meant files for the bars, opiates for the jailers, and a coach in waiting.

Some say that Law made straight for France, some say the Netherlands; all we know for certain is that the next ten years were spent in travel—Amsterdam, St Germain-en-Laye, Neuchâtel, Genoa, Venice, Turin, and even his native Scotland, for Scotland still preserved her separate government, and he was free there from apprehension for offences committed in England.

He was a rake and a gambler, but a rake devoted to his mistress and their children, a gambler who played coolly and skilfully—and always won.

For Law was a financial genius. Throughout his wanderings he produced a series of pamphlets and memoranda on state banks, credit, and the use of paper money, and by 1720 he had been pardoned by George III, given the freedom of his native Edinburgh in a silver box, was a millionaire, a naturalized Frenchman, Minister of Finance to the duke of Orleans (regent in the name of the infant Louis XV) and, as projector of France's first system of paper currency and author of the 'Mississippi scheme' for colonizing France's Louisiana territory, the most talked-of man in Europe.

This is not the place in which to follow the fantastic switchback of Law's fortunes.[6] It is enough to know that when he died, less than ten years later, 'in a tawdry Venice lodging house', to quote Mr Montgomery Hyde, 'nearly destitute and largely for-

[5] 'The appeal was in the nature of a private action between the parties by which, if the case went against the defendant, and the plaintiff insisted on it, the death of the deceased was to be compensated for by the death of the defendant. In such a case the Crown could not remit judgement, and the law had to take its course in the shape of the defendant's execution.' H. Montgomery Hyde, *John Law: the History of an Honest Adventurer*, London 1948.

[6] The interested inquirer is referred to H. Montgomery Hyde's book, to the *Dictionary of National Biography*, and to *The Cambridge Modern History*, volume VI, chapter VI.

gotten', his estate in France, such as it was, could not go to his own children, for they were illegitimate, but went to the two infant sons of his brother William, born French citizens.

William Law had been his elder brother's agent in London, and joined him in Paris not only to act as his assistant in the management of the bank he had established there, but to take over with him the Birmingham clockmakers and other craftsmen whose skills John Law proposed to introduce into France.

For some complicated financial reason, William had already been assigned the Lauriston estates, and he and his family took the name with them to France without Frenchifying it—all that happened was that the 'of' became 'de', but it denoted a family of Scottish, not of French, descent.

William's elder son, Jean Law de Lauriston, born in 1729, the year his famous uncle died, became governor of Pondicherry; one of his sons was an A.D.C. to Napoleon, carried to London the terms of the Treaty of Amiens, and became a Marshal of France; another, Louis-Georges, held high civilian office under Napoleon, and his son married a daughter of the Marquis de Boubers; the family settled in Touraine. Louis-Georges's grandson, Olivier, was a cavalry officer and a country gentleman: his daughter, Elisabeth ('Lily') de Lauriston, born on 1 October 1899, married in 1923 Jacques Bollinger, grandson of the original Joseph-Jacob-Placide Bollinger.

The bridegroom had become head of the firm in 1918, on the death of his father, actually taking over control on his demobilization from the French Air Force the following year, only twenty-four, but already decorated with the Légion d'Honneur and the Croix de Guerre with palms.

When the Second World War broke out, Jacques Bollinger, as an officer in the reserve, was recalled to the Air Force, but he was a sick man, and was put on to the retired list in December 1939. He took up, instead, what can hardly have been less onerous: the mayoralty of his native town under German occupation. (His father, not as mayor but as a municipal councillor of Ay, had had a similarly heart-breaking job in 1914: as we have seen, his great-grandfather, the admiral, saved Ay from being despoiled by the Russians in 1814.)

He died, untimely, in 1941, having already expressed the wish that his widow should take up the reins.

Naturally, after nearly twenty years of marriage, he had known her character and her quality. But he also appreciated what she knew about champagne and how to taste it, for he had coached her himself.

Madame Bollinger had grown up in Touraine, in a handsome house in a sizeable estate (and, as a matter of course, with an English governess: she speaks admirable English). But its vineyards were simply, as it were, home-farm vineyards—they produced modest *vins ordinaires* for the family's own meals and for the staff: not even such as the family would offer to guests.

Then, in 1923, she married not only a dashing young wartime airman and peacetime sportsman of twenty-eight or so—she married a great wine.

For keen as her young husband was on his fishing and sailing, his riding and his shooting (a favourite family sport: boar's heads bare their tusks at you in the hall of Madame Bollinger's house, victims of various male Bollingers), he was dedicated to his wine. Madame Bollinger has described how he used to cross-examine her: which of these vintages did she prefer? Why this one rather than that? And described, too, how eagerly she learned.

It was a tough job she took over, at a tough time. The Germans carried off most of the best wines in the cellars, and required a yearly levy. Eventually, Bollinger, with the other champagne houses, were permitted to export wine to Switzerland, the Netherlands and Italy, as well as to sell in France, but the best of all markets, Britain and the United States were, of course, closed.

Meanwhile, there were no able-bodied men for the vineyards, little or no fertilizers and chemicals for the vines. No petrol, either. This was the time that Madame Bollinger took to the bicycle: she has ridden one pretty well every working day of the thirty years since then.

She and her one servant slept in the cellars as the allied bombings heralded the allied armies, and it was from the Bollinger cellars, one early morning, that she stepped out to greet the liberators.

Another cyclist of the time was M. Yves Moret de Rocheprise,

Jacques Bollinger's cousin. His father, who had been a director of the firm, was a grandson of the original Bollinger through the female line, and thus Yves is a direct descendant of both Joseph-Jacques-Bollinger and of Amiral Comte de Villermont, the founders of the firm.

M. de Rocheprise was unfit for war service, and also happened, when petrol became unobtainable, to be already the owner of a bicycle. So he took over superintendence of the vineyards themselves, to give Madame Bollinger, though she also had an eye to the vineyards, time too for the cellars, the tasting-room, the account books and the occupying authorities. Now, when he takes you round the vineyards, obviously immensely knowledgeable about the vines and the pests and diseases that can afflict them, and about the vignerons, their virtues and their failings, he explains that he learned all this by having to do it: 'You see, I had a bicycle.'

M. Yves de Rocheprise is now a director—and inevitably the director responsible for vineyards.

Madame Bollinger has two younger sisters, Madame Bizot and Madame de Valbray. Madame Bizot's son, Christian, is a director of the firm—in charge of sales, both at home and abroad—and so is Claude d'Hautefeuille, married to Madame de Valbray's daughter, Claire. M. Bizot was too young for the war, but M. d'Hautefeuille, a professional soldier, was a colonel in the Foreign Legion and made a daring escape from hospital after being badly wounded—it was thought mortally—in the last desperate fighting before the Germans broke through to Paris. Madame d'Hautefeuille was in the Resistance as a girl of twenty; was arrested and sent to a German jail; her brother died in a concentration camp.

Three of the four directors of Bollinger, therefore—Madame Bollinger herself, her nephew and her nephew by marriage—are direct descendants of William Law of Lauriston, and collateral descendants of John Law himself, 'the Projector'. The fourth is a direct descendant of the original Bollinger. The board is constructed like this:

Madame Jacques Bollinger: *Président Directeur-Général*;

M. Claude d'Hautefeuille:	*Président Directeur-Général Adjoint,* generally responsible for administration;
M. Yves de Rocheprise:	*Directeur-Général Adjoint,* in charge of vineyards;
M. Christian Bizot:	*Directeur,* in charge of sales.

It is a family-owned, family-controlled, private company, cherishing its independence. As M. Christian Bizot once put it to me: 'Making champagne isn't the same as making shoe-laces, you know; the maker's personality decides the style of the wine, and the personality and the style are reflected in what people today call "the brand-image". If a maker's his own boss, then both the style and the image are safe.'

The four directors all live so close to each other in Ay that each could very nearly invite another to dinner merely by opening a window and raising his voice. The vines come almost up to the walls of their houses, as they do in fact to those of the firm's headquarters, a great nineteenth-century pile with three miles of cellars cut into the chalk beneath. One entrance to the cellars is here, under the headquarters, where the reception-room and board-room, offices and tasting-room are. The other is through the press-house immediately across the Rue Jules-Lobet—too narrow, really, to be dignified with the name *rue*—from Madame Bollinger's house.

Thus, though it is a dignified eighteenth-century house she lives in, with panelled rooms and a prettily curving staircase—long, low, grey-shuttered, with something of the air of a country manor house, for all that it stands (behind its high courtyard walls) in the street—Madame Bollinger could boast, were she given to boasting, that she lives over the shop. The house constitutes one side of the paved and gravelled courtyard in which stand oleanders in massive tubs; on the other sides are the street wall and gates; what used to be a cooperage, now a place where casks are stored and repaired, but no longer made; and yet another entrance to the cellars. Madame Bollinger can actually see the houses of M. Bizot and M. d'Hautefeuille from her own:

this is a curiously close-knit family, geographically as in every other way.

Come to luncheon here, and you find a typical country-house gentlewoman—a sturdily-built, but young-faced seventy-year-old lady, tweed-suited, or twin-setted, or silk-frocked, according to season (the suits and the frocks are by Jacques Heim)—perhaps putting down her petit-point embroidery as you arrive, or the stamp album she has been explaining to a couple or so of her nineteen nephews and nieces, sixty-three great-nephews and great-nieces. If you did not know her, you might think that nothing much else crops up in a long, unhurried day but a consultation with the cook, another with the gardener, and half an hour in the flower-room, unless she has arranged a day in Paris, to visit her dressmaker.

In fact, your hostess is a working-woman: she works in the vineyards, as a sort of super-inspector; in the tasting-room (as will be seen in a later chapter) very much as the head of Bollinger's tasting panel; in the board-room very much as the policy-making head of a great firm; and abroad, wherever Bollinger is sold, as Bollinger's ambassadress, flying to New York and across the United States as nonchalantly and as frequently as another septuagenarian *champenoise* might take a train for a holiday on the Côte d'Azur. This is the Président Directeur-Général who built up Bollinger's sales from half a million to a million bottles a year; this is the first and only woman ever to be invited as a guest at the great banquet held every year in London, since 1888, by the Wine and Spirit Trades' Benevolent Society, which she was in 1969, to receive a standing ovation from 1,100 male fellow-diners, a most moving occasion to all who love good wine and the men—and women—who make it.

A story of Mr Patrick Forbes's sums up something of Madame Bollinger's quality:

Well do I remember how, at a large dinner-party which she gave in her home for a group of young British wine merchants, she handed round the coffee, the *marc* and the cognac herself, letting drop as she did so that she had been out since six in the morning inspecting the vines. The hour was very late; it would have been easy for the servants who had served the delicious dinner to serve the coffee and the *digestifs* too; but when you are young, and when you yourself were still in bed at eight or nine, it is quite something to have been offered your coffee and your *marc* or your cognac by a great lady of Champagne who was out in the vineyards at six.

5. Violence in the Vineyards

As typically *champenois* as the Bollinger family is that of Maurice Renoir, seventy-five years old, whom I met when he called at the Bollinger offices in Ay, on a little matter of business. For M. Renoir had recently swopped a family vineyard of about an acre in Verzenay, where the Renoirs had lived for longer than records go back, for a similar piece in Ay, owned by Bollinger, but not quite fitting geographically into the other Bollinger properties there, whereas the Verzenay parcel did. There are many of these small exchanges in Champagne between one great house and another that own vineyards, and between great houses and small grower-proprietors, as in this one between Bollinger and M. Renoir.

Lean and bright-eyed—'you see how champagne keeps you fit', he says—M. Renoir fought at Verdun in the First World War, and can put up the Médaille Militaire and the Croix de Guerre when he parades with his comrade-contemporaries on Quatorze Juillet. He is just as proud, though, of being '*tout champenois*': his father and all the forebears he has ever heard of were vignerons; one brother grows grapes at Verzenay, where the family comes from, another is head vigneron to the *grande marque* firm of Lanson at Dizy, and his forty-seven-year-old son holds a similar job with Roederer, an especially distinguished house, at Chouilly. He himself once worked on a vineyard belonging to Heidsieck Dry Monopole, has lived at Ay for the past quarter of a century, and although the one-acre vineyard there is now his own property, the 100-per-cent category Pinot Noir grapes[1] he grows on it are all sold to Bollinger, its former owners.

He drinks more champagne in a year than many a rich Englishman or American does—a bottle a week, at least, thanks to the tradition that vineyard workers and vineyard-owners are supplied by the firms they work for or sell to (M. Renoir would have to own five times as big a vineyard to be able to make his own), to say nothing of special occasions such as the St Vincent banquet, the feast at the end of the vintage, St John's Day, Christmas, and various family festivities.

Multiply this by his more than sixty years' experience of growing and of drinking champagne—he began working in the vineyards at thirteen for his father, who made his own wine—and one realizes that here is a man who has forgotten more about champagne than many a *bon vivant* in St James's or Park Avenue or the more fashionable *faubourgs* has ever known.

M. Renoir well remembers the wines made before the vineyards of Champagne were devastated by the plague of phylloxera —the plant louse that kills the vine at the root. Indeed, he can remember the plague itself, for it came later there than to Spain and Italy, Bordeaux and Burgundy. Long before it was noticed in Champagne for the first time, in 1890, it had already cost France more than twice the indemnity exacted by Germany after the war of 1870. (Before it was finally routed it was costing the French wine-growers £50 million a year.) When it did reach Champagne it spread more slowly, because of the region's cooler climate. In 1892, there were five acres of vineyards affected in the Marne; by 1910, when Maurice Renoir was already working among the vines, it was 16,000 acres—virtually half the vineyards of the region.

Eventually, the answer to the phylloxera plague was to graft the 'noble' vines of France—the vines, that is, that are the only ones permitted to make the classic wines—on to phylloxera-

---

[1] For the principle of price categorization, see chapter 7.

resistant American stocks. All the great vines of the world now grow from American roots.

But wines were being made from the old French vines until well after the First World War, and M. Renoir remembers them as being a deeper gold in colour than those of today, with more body and bouquet. He hastens to explain that this is not nostalgia speaking: that there is reason for this having been so—the yield to the acre was less, the grapes were smaller, and they were trained nearer to the ground. More grape-skin to less juice, from grapes ripened more thoroughly by reflection of heat from the ground, from which a smaller crop than today's would draw proportionately more nutriment—all this would, indeed, mean more colour, fuller flavour, and a more concentrated fragrance.

All the same, those were the bad old days, and M. Renoir goes on to explain that times were hard then, that the wines, though splendid at their best, were woefully inconsistent, that some makers defrauded their customers, and that some exploited their workers. The new, grafted, vines produce a better yield and more consistent wine, and fraud and exploitation have become unknown, he says, since the riots of 1911.

He came back constantly in his conversation to these disturbances, and so did everyone else I spoke to in Champagne— grower and maker—whenever I asked about the official control of quality of the wine and whenever I asked about working conditions in particular and about standards of life in general.

The riots of 1911 loom as large, almost, in the minds of the middle-aged and the elderly *champenois* as the two great world wars that have swept across the Marne valley and its downlands. Especially, they are important to the people of Ay, and they are significant to anyone wishing to understand Bollinger's prestige in the region.

*   *   *

La belle époque was not so beautiful a period for the French peasants and urban workers as for the captains of industry and the gentlemen of the Jockey Club, and for the parfumiers, couturiers and restaurateurs who lapped their wives and their mistresses in luxury.

In Champagne, particularly, times were bad in the decade before the Kaiser's uhlans jingled in from the east.

Although eventually the answer to the phylloxera was to graft on to American stock, the immediate counter-measure was to spray with carbon disulphide, an unpleasant and a very expensive process.

Few of the small growers could afford it, and a fund was opened, with contributions from the government, local chambers of commerce, and the big champagne houses, to make it available to them. Such, though, was the suspicion of the big champagne firms entertained by the small peasant farmers that one out of three refused to co-operate.

The suspicion was understandable, though it was by no means always justifiable.

The great prosperity of the champagne trade throughout the nineteenth century, and particularly towards its end, had attracted new men with new business methods into the region—men to whom it was an article of faith, adhered to with more than religious zeal, that one sold in the dearest and bought in the cheapest market.

They were in the minority: as we have seen, there were many great houses, Bollinger among them, with reputations as high as their histories were long. But even a few of the get-rich-quick firms could cause great mischief. This they did by strict adherence to their article of faith.

The cheapest market for new wine from which sparkling wine of a sort could be made in the cellars and sold from the offices that such people had acquired in Reims and Epernay was certainly not the great vignoble that surrounded these towns: it was France's deep south. Warner Allen, who became later, between the wars, one of Britain's leading amateurs of, and writers about, wine was then the Paris correspondent of the *Morning Post*. A story he told in the 18 January 1911 issue of his paper, to explain the troubles that were then beginning, in a despatch headed, 'Unrest in the Champagne Country', sums it all up:

The chief complaint in this district is that the Champagne firms purchase wines outside the district and, after giving them the main characteristics of true champagne, sell them as the

V   The Champagne Riots, 1911
(a) Demonstrators on the march.
(b) The women of Ay in action against the cavalry.

VI The Champagne Riots, 1911
    (a) Incendiarism at Maison
    Geldermann, next door
    to Bollinger.

(b) Vignerons man the barricades.

I(a) Pruning the vines in winter is a highly skilled task. The method of pruning a classic vine is laid down by law.

(b) Helicopter spraying against mildew, when rains have made the ground too heavy for tractors.

VIII   Jeroboams *en pupitre*.

genuine wine. There is undoubtedly truth in their complaint. A friend of mine who is the proprietor of a vineyard producing an inferior wine not in the Champagne district, hit on the idea of sending his vintage to one of the great Champagne firms, which in return sends him so many dozen bottles of champagne specially labelled with his name as the brand. 'Of course,' he explained, 'the wine I get is not really from my grapes. The whole of my vintage goes into the great vats of the firm and is mixed with all kinds of other vintages, and the wine they send is, except for the label, exactly what they usually sell.'

(In 1924, in his *The Wines of France*, Warner Allen rather more precisely identified the 'friend of mine . . . producing an inferior wine not in the Champagne district' as 'a rich French youth who owned a vineyard somewhere in the Midi', and his grapes as 'very inferior'.)

This was no new thing. An association of vignerons had been founded in 1904 to try, with the help of the reputable, old-established champagne firms, to bring pressure on to the government to protect the grower of the grapes, the maker of honest wine and the drinker of champagne, the one from being exploited, the second from unfair competition, the third from being deceived.

It took until the end of 1908 for legislation to be introduced, delimiting those areas where the vineyards were entitled to call their wines champagne. It was ill-conceived as to the boundaries, and it was feeble as to the means of enforcement, but all might have been put right by peaceable discussion had it not been that the phylloxera scourge and the two bad vintages of 1907 and 1908 were followed by the equally bad vintage of 1909 and the completely disastrous one of 1910. The vignerons were in despair: all were in debt, and many faced bankruptcy.

In spite of the decree of December 1908, more and more wine from other parts of France found its way into the vats of the Champagne region. It was no longer being sneaked in, it was pouring in, is the way a French pamphlet put it. Indeed, it was as much because of the decree as in spite of it that this was happening, because once the measure began to be publicly discussed, and before it was signed, the less scrupulous champagne-makers bought as much wine as they could from wherever it was to be found, hoping—with good grounds for their optimism—that what was already in the region when the decree was signed would have to be regarded as champagne.

Then, when it was realized that the machinery for enforcing the decree was quite inadequate, the champagne-makers (one is tempted to call them the champagne-fakers) carried on as openly as before.

It was too much for the vignerons. There had already been sporadic meetings and demonstrations for a couple of years past —one such had seen ten thousand farmers marching in good order through Epernay—and threats of withholding taxes, which in those days were levied not on the harvest but on the land.

It is well to remember that ours is not, as some would have us suppose, the only period of peacetime demonstrations and violence. Not even the only such period in the twentieth century. Here in Britain, at the time of which we write, in 1910 and 1911, troops were called out against rioting coalminers in the Rhondda and the Aberdare valleys, against dockers in the north, where men were shot dead, and in Llanelly, where again they opened fire. In London, suffragettes were breaking windows and battering cabinet ministers, and at the 'Siege' of Sidney Street in January 1911 troops fired to kill for the first time in the capital since the Cato Street conspiracy of 1820. Abroad there were anarchist demonstrations in New York, and disturbances in St Petersburg and Tokyo.

In Paris there had been *apache* and anarchist outrages, and— how familiar it sounds!—the police had made arrests when student demonstrations at the Sorbonne spilled into the streets.

The Radical Clemenceau had spent most of his years as prime minister, 1906 to 1909, in slapping down strikers and repressing disorder, not scrupling to use troops in doing so. When the wine-growers of the Languedoc, suffering from a combination of over-production and Algerian competition, took to rioting, the 17th Infantry mutinied rather than fire on their fellow-countrymen.

So violence was in the air of France, as of other countries. Already, as we have seen, some of the demonstrators in Champagne had marched to its very brink. Now, the vignerons would not be restrained, and on 17 January 1911, learning that a truck with 'foreign' wine was on its way to Epernay, those in the riverside villages rose to a tocsin of bells, bugles and hail-rockets,[2] and marched, some two or three thousand strong, under the red flag, to sack the cellars of an unpopular champagne-maker in Damery, a pretty village some three or four miles from Epernay on the other side of the Marne. They smashed the bottles in the cellars and stove in the casks, wrecked the presses and flung a waggon and its load of bottles into the river. Thousands of pounds' worth of damage was done in an hour of the mid-afternoon: by the time the police and the local officials had arrived, everyone was back at his home; nobody talked, not even at the Town Hall enquiry held next day by the public prosecutor.

It was the beginning of some four months of virtual insurrection, and nine months of military occupation.

For the events of the afternoon set off similar events that night at Hautvillers, and this time authority moved.

Since long before 1870, and with all the more reason since, Champagne had been, and still was, one of the most heavily garrisoned regions of France. The 31st Regiment of Dragoons, issued with carbines and small-arms ammunition in addition to its great cavalry sabres, trotted out from Epernay, helmeted and breastplated, to watch the roads into the town, to guard the railway station, where wine was still arriving from the south, and to protect those champagne houses that were in the greatest danger, or that considered themselves to be, and could make their apprehensions felt—those, perhaps, with the guiltiest consciences.

Two battalions of the line marched into the district, together with seven squadrons from the 5th and the 15th Regiments of Chasseurs à Cheval—light cavalry. They were split up between Epernay itself and the string of villages and small towns across

[2] For a few years, at this time, a specially designed gun was used that fired a rocket into the clouds to disperse a possible hail-storm. It was not very good at this particular job (though it is still used in other parts of France), but came in useful as a call to arms.

the river, along the vineyards of the Vallée de la Marne: Venteuil, Damery, Cumières, Hautvillers. In Ay there were a battalion of infantry and a squadron of cavalry—perhaps the better part of a thousand men, in a town the population of which in those days was probably not much more than three or four times as much.

The prime minister, Aristide Briand (to be succeeded by the time of the riots in Ay by 'the inoffensive and ineffective M. Monis'),[3] made it clear to the local authorities that arrests were to be avoided lest worse befall and, in spite of the presence of the troops, meetings and demonstrations continued, with the walls at Bouzy and at Rilly being plastered with posters proclaiming this champagne-shipper to be a Jew, that to be a traitor, the other to be a poisoner. Supplies of wine were intercepted and sent back to the Midi; casks in other consignments were smashed and topped up with paraffin.

The government had to act, and on 11 February 1911 the Senate ratified a measure stringently controlling the making and marketing of champagne, and rendering it virtually impossible to pass off as champagne sparkling wines made out of wine from other regions. Basically, the law was sound, and remedied known abuses. But it had been hastily drafted and some of the people concerned had been ill-prepared for it.

In the Marne, anyway, it was rapturously welcomed. Down came the red flag, and up went the tricolour; in the streets, which were decked with bunting, the girls danced with the soldiers; on hastily erected platforms local bigwigs made complimentary speeches to the officers before they marched their men back to barracks.

Too soon.

In the delimitation of the region necessary as its framework, the new law of February 1911 excluded an outlying wine-growing area in the *département* of the Aube, south-east of the classic Marne region and separated from it by some forty miles or so of

[3] The phrase is that of Professor D. W. Brogan, *The Development of Modern France (1870–1939)*, London, 1940. Monis was in office only from March to the end of June 1911, preceded by Aristide Briand and succeeded by Joseph Caillaux.

largely dairy-farming country between the Aube and the upper reaches of the Seine.

The *aubois* stoutly maintained that they ought to be included: the *département* had always been part of the historic county and province of Champagne, of which its chief town, Troyes, had once been the capital. Their wines could not compete in Paris with those of the Midi: their only market was the champagne industry of Reims and Epernay.

The area had been excluded from the delimited champagne region in the legislation of 1908, and there had been rumblings then, but nothing more than that because it had been pretty clear that the law was not going to be observed, and could not be enforced.

The law of February 1911 was a tougher proposition altogether, and this time there was more than rumbling in the Aube.

Up went not only the red flag, but the black flag, too. Eight thousand wine-growers, baskets on back, hoes at the slope, marched through the streets of Bar-sur-Aube, headed by two bands, the fire brigade—so essential a part of all French provincial life and public display—and the mayors and the curés of the towns and villages around, and, to the strains of the 'Internationale' and 'La Carmagnole', solemnly set fire first to the tax assessment forms with which their baskets had been loaded and then to an effigy of M. Monis. Thirty-six mayors then resigned their offices.

It did not take much of this sort of thing in Bar-sur-Aube, Troyes and the rest of the region to bustle poor M. Monis into another hasty, ill-considered measure. On 11 April 1911 the government announced its intention of annulling the delimiting laws of 1908 and 1911, thus 'abandoning the territorial delimitations which may provoke divisions among Frenchmen', putting an end to discrimination against the Aube wines, and permitting their growers to call them champagne or, at any rate, ceasing to forbid them to do so. Thus, it was hoped, there would be an end to the disturbances in those parts.

What it ensured, of course, was a renewed and much more violent outbreak in the Marne, where the vignerons, quite rightly, regarded their wines as enormously superior to those of the

Aube, and feared, also with some justice, that if champagne-makers in the Marne could import wines from the Aube that would have to come by train from outside their own compact region, it was thus made all the easier for the unscrupulous to import wines of even lower quality from even further afield.

The men of the Marne were all the more furiously indignant because what had been given by one hand—the integrity of their wines—was now being taken away by another, and after so short a time. Violence clearly paid: it had paid them in February, now in April it had paid the *aubois*.

News of the government's decision reached Epernay at five in the afternoon, and bugles and bells, rockets, hail guns and bon-fires roused what next morning's outraged French and British newspapers referred to variously as 'the mob' and '*la jacquerie*'. Before dusk, the vignerons were on the march, armed with hoes and mattocks, vine-props and barrel-staves, sporting guns, bottles and hatchets, to sack Dizy and Damery. As night fell, the smashing into cellars and houses, the breaking of bottles and of furniture, the broaching of casks, went on by torchlight, which flickered on the wine running down the streets.

Out came the military again; in some places, the cavalry charged with sabres drawn; in others, women threw themselves down before the horses and inhibited any action.

Next morning, troops continued to pour into Epernay, aug-menting the garrison there, and filling the riverside villages—some 20,000 of them, mostly cavalry. At the same time cyclists from Epernay and Ay carried, as it were, the fiery cross into every village of the Montagne, the Vallée and the Côte.

'From the western slopes of the Montagne de Reims', wrote the correspondent hurriedly despatched to Epernay from the Paris office of *The Times*, 'there swooped down upon the valley some 10,000 or 12,000 peasant vine-dressers, sturdy knaves armed with bludgeons.' (There is no mistaking where the sym-pathies of the French and the British press lay. Warner Allen, too, writing for the *Morning Post*, took at first a view so reactionary as to be positively wall-eyed, though he changed his tune in a book written later.)

It is estimated that there were some six thousand men and

women from fifty villages milling around in Ay alone. Most were genuinely indignant vignerons and their wives, but there were undoubtedly some landless men too, on the look-out for trouble —and for loot.

This is where the greatest damage was done, and this is the little town that gives its name to what are still referred to, if not as the Champagne riots, then as the Ay riots.

In a way, it was unintentional: Ay was not the object of the demonstration as originally planned.

Rather after midday on 12 April, about fifteen hundred of the rioters in Ay, where a squadron of light cavalry (some hundred and twenty men or so) had moved in that morning, to relieve a squadron of dragoons, set off to link up with five or six hundred men from Dizy to march on Epernay.

Orders to the military from Paris and from Reims had been that Epernay was to be saved at all costs, and there were now no fewer than six squadrons of cavalry there, as well as infantry. The major commanding the cavalry in Ay had put barricades across the roads leading to Epernay, and he held them. Thwarted, the crowd of vignerons turned back into the centre of Ay down a parallel road, and the cavalry was prevented by its own barricades, and by the way the streets ran, from outflanking the vignerons and containing them. Infantry could have done it, but the infantry did not arrive until all was over.

The rioters, denied Epernay, set to work on Ay. They threw up barricades of their own—waggons, railings, chains, ropes and bottles, empty and full. The cavalry tried another road to turn their flank, and found themselves in a sunken street between buildings on one side and high vineyards supported by retaining walls on another. From these, rocks and full champagne bottles were hurled down at them, mostly by women, whose men got to work in the buildings and the cellars, though there were women too in the offices, playing hell with the books.

A subaltern asked for permission to open fire, but the major refused it: at one point, though, dismounted *chasseurs à cheval* were whacking at rioters with the flats of their sabres, themselves under a rain of stones and bottles.

Three more troops of cavalry moved in, but infantry would

have been more useful: street-fighting is a specialized trade, and horse-soldiers are not schooled in it.

The mob was into the Ayala building now; into Deutz and Geldermann; into Bissinger. It was monstrously unfair. The rioters were in Ay only because they had been prevented from marching on Epernay, and they were in these houses only because these houses were unprotected. The reason they were unprotected was that they were those of firms that had not been guilty of the frauds that so incensed the vignerons, were known not to be guilty, and who felt, therefore, that they were in no danger and needed no protection, such as some of their rivals had demanded of the troops and of the police.

By now, in any case, as a French historian of the troubles points out, 'the crowd was over-excited. It was tired; it had been on its feet since early morning. There was an atmosphere of civil war. Men and women had eaten too little and drunk too much . . . there had been sound and fury.'

And so it was that the Ayala, Deutz and Geldermann, and Bissinger establishments were not only sacked but set alight. And not only the business places—poor Madame Bissinger's own house was burned down, paintings torn from the wall and hacked to pieces before being put on a bonfire, her jewellery and plate made away with.

All the same, one house was spared. About fifteen years later, as Madame Bollinger has told me, she was standing by a window of her house in Ay, and heard a passer-by point it out to his companion, saying, 'That's the Bollinger house, you know: we didn't touch it during the riots here—as a matter of fact, we lowered our flag to it as we passed!' 'Probably the red flag,' Madame adds, with pleased irony. Still, not a finger was laid on a single brick in the Bollinger building, or bottle in the Bollinger cellars.

To this day, as I found in my conversation with Maurice Renoir, the *champenois* cite the clemency shown to Bollinger as evidence of the reasonableness in their fathers' rioting—a well-deserved tribute to Bollinger's integrity, but rather hard on other Ay firms that were equally scrupulous, the premises of which were gutted just the same. It may be that particularly strict injunctions had gone forth from the leaders of the mob—in so

far as there were leaders, and in so far as they had any authority—
that Bollinger in particular was to be respected.

* * *

As the fires burned down, so did the ardour of the rioters.
Infantry moved in from Epernay, which they had been helping to
guard all day, and where there had been some disturbances, not
to mention a sabre charge in which dragoons were unhorsed, but
far less damage than at Ay. As the troops moved in, vignerons
and less respectable rioters moved out, the vignerons to go home,
some of the others, no doubt, to look elsewhere for loot.

Warner Allen was in the district that evening for the *Morning
Post:*

From Epernay I drove to Ay, where the rioters had worked
their will unchecked for hours. A whole row of houses in the
north-east corner—the warehouses and cellars of champagne
merchants—had been absolutely gutted. At the corner four
roofless smoke-grimed walls marked all that remained of the
warehouse of MM. Bissinger and a house attached to it.
Everything inside had been wrecked, and fire had done the
rest. Troops and firemen were at work knocking down danger-
ous pieces of masonry, and sentinels barred the little crowd of
sightseers from the road.

A path, however, through the vineyards up to the sunny
slopes above the ruined houses enables the sightseer to evade
the vigilance of the soldiers and have a clear view of the scene
of desolation. At once one understood why the squadron of
Dragoons[4] had been compelled to stand by helpless. They
could drive the rioters from the street, but it was impossible
to follow them into the vine-clad hills which command this
corner of the village. All the vineyards are covered with stacks
of vine props which provided formidable weapons, and when
the Cavalry attempted to gain a footing on the friable soil they

[4] In fact, *chasseurs*. The 31st Dragoons had left at dawn, and throughout
the day the only troops in Ay were a squadron each of the 15th and the 22nd
Chasseurs à Cheval. Dragoons were just outside the town, guarding the road
to Epernay.

were driven back by showers of stones. Infantry alone could have acted with any effect.

From the slope above the smoking ruins of one house and the collapsing roof from which the zinc had melted with the heat of another was melancholy proof of the vignerons' madness. The ventilating shafts of the cellars had been madly attacked, the solid masonry which protected them torn from its place, and hurled down upon the iron bars below. Hundreds of vines which had just begun to bud had been trodden under foot and ruined, while the ground was strewn with broken bottles, many of them from their labels having contained vintage wines. In the road below, iron hoops, huge barrels, account books and ledgers were scattered in indescribable confusion, all sodden with the wine which filled the air with its fumes. A cellar-man who had endeavoured to protect his master's property—as a bandaged head betokened—was trying to save a few papers from the wreck. At Ay alone five warehouses and as many private houses have been sacked and burnt and some five or six million bottles destroyed.

Sporadic rioting went on for another couple of days at various villages in the Montagne, the Vallée and the Côte, but it was pretty well all over. *L'Humanité* reported that there were more soldiers than vignerons in Champagne. One report had it that there were more than 40,000, horse and foot, which may have been an exaggeration, but there were certainly two of a new sort of fighting man: 'two Army airmen descended upon Epernay in monoplanes out of the clouds yesterday', the special correspondent of *The Times* reported. (It was less than a couple of years since Blériot had flown the Channel: can this have been the first use of heavier-than-air craft in a warlike or quasi-warlike operation?)

But by 15 April, in addition to the substantial garrison in Epernay, there were thirty-one squadrons of cavalry and twenty-six companies of infantry billeted on the inhabitants of the strictly wine-growing area of Montagne, Vallée and Côte, which was split into seven military zones of occupation, each under a colonel, with a major-general over all.

It was not entirely the military occupation that brought the uproar to an end. The vignerons had let off steam, and now they were rather running out of it. They may have felt that the government would act again, as it had acted before, when told vociferously enough that action was expected. They may have been a little shaken to see what they had done: more than a million pounds' worth of damage, was one contemporary estimate, and a million pounds meant much more then that it does now. What is more, it was damage to their own livelihoods—presses and bottling plants; bottles and casks and vats, vines, props and protective matting.

It is astonishing that only one man lost his life in the actual rioting and clashes with the troops[5]—a M. Thuiller of Ay, who suffered 'bruised kidneys'—an unfortunate diagnosis for a battered butcher—but whose death was put down at the inquest to 'natural causes'. Two vignerons, though, hanged themselves before they could be brought to trial in the course of the savage repression that followed: they were certain they would be sent to prison, and prison was a disgrace, even for an offence in which all one's friends and neighbours had shared.

Some rioters had been arrested during the disturbances and kept under military guard, awaiting trial. As the troubles died down, the police more than made up for any lack of zeal they had shown during the actual riots. They arrested literally hundreds—some they had remembered themselves as having seen in action; some they had been told about and some on information received in anonymous letters. Some were identified in the flickering newsreel that the manager of the Pathé cinema in Epernay projected over and over again for their benefit, among them one man eventually sent down for four months for striking horses with a vine prop, another the same sentence for shaking his fist at an officer. . . .

Cases were dealt with summarily at Reims and Epernay; more serious charges went to Douai assizes; some went to the court of appeal, where without exception, to the indignation even of those newspapers that had called for the exemplary punishment of the

[5] And, so far as I can discover, one troop horse, killed in Epernay by a home-made bomb. The dragoon was badly, but not fatally, injured.

rioters, sentences were increased. A boy of twelve was sent to prison for three weeks for drinking a glass of looted wine, and the girl of fifteen who gave it to him was sentenced to a month.

Curiously, the man whom many had regarded as the ring-leader, forty-year-old Emile Michel-Lecacheur, charged as an accessory to the looting, was acquitted. He was comfortably off, a considerable landowner, an officer in the reserve, and politically right-wing, but had identified himself with the small vignerons, and loudly voiced their grievances.

He made no bones about having been present at the Ay riots and he spoke out stoutly in court against the fakers and on be-half of the growers. Witnesses differed as to whether he had attempted to restrain the rioters or to encourage them, but those who spoke against him showed obvious malice, and the judges gave him the benefit of the doubt.

。　*　　　*　　　*

There were those who saw a vast international anarchist plot and foreign money behind the disturbances, as there are those today who see a communist under every bed, clutching a bag of Russian gold. There was a serious anarchist movement in France in those days, with its own newspapers, and some active anarch-ists had undoubtedly gone specially to Champagne during the disturbances: they would have been pretty feeble anarchists had they not. But such known anarchist leaders as were charged with conspiracy were acquitted: there had been no plot. What there had been was genuine grievance; active anarchists moved in only after this had broken out into demonstrations.

One curious touch is that in some places, notably in the Aube, during the demonstrations there, the German flag was run up, either alongside red flags and black flags, or instead of them. There seems to have been no political reason for this: it was merely the most obvious way in which rather simple Frenchmen could display their disgust with a French government.

It accords oddly, though, with the presence on the scene of one who was to be shot at Vincennes in 1917 for 'treasonable conspiracy' in having received nearly half a million pounds from German emissaries in order to buy Paris newspapers and spread defeatism through them: the bizarre Bolo Pasha, millionaire swindler, white-slave trader, blackmailer and bigamist. Until he was found out, Bolo Pasha was an important figure, with fingers in many pies—a sort of exotic Horatio Bottomley—and in 1911, amongst many other offices, he was president of a national body for the protection of pure food and its producers, to which a vignerons' federation was affiliated. He bustled about, talking to bigwigs, but seems to have used his influence on the side of moderation.

It is clear now that there was no need to look for foreign gold and professional agitators. There had perhaps been a certain amount of fraud throughout the nineteenth century, in the addition to champagne of wine made out of grapes from other regions. But it had not been on a great scale, and the vignerons of the Marne were doing well enough anyway.

Then came the phylloxera, four successive bad vintages—and an increased demand for champagne. This made fraud more profitable for the new big-business makers of champagne, more disastrous for the growers. As soon as their representations led to the possibility of government measures, there was a rush to stock up warehouses and cellars with wines from the Loire and the Midi; the vignerons became angrier than ever; and their anger was exacerbated by the shifts and changes of mind of government. Moreover, as we have already noticed, violence was in the air and in the fashion.

*   *   *

'But what good came of it at last?'
Quoth little Peterkin . . .

Generally speaking, the property-owning classes, who had been talking in their drawing-rooms of a rising of the *jacquerie*, or writing, in the columns of *The Times*, of 'sturdy knaves armed with bludgeons', came to realize as the trials went on that there were genuine grievances in the vineyards, and that on the whole it had been responsible men—themselves peasant proprietors—who had been pushed beyond endurance.

They even came to understand what the grievances were. It

is instructive to compare Warner Allen writing from Paris in January 1911, at the very beginning of the disturbances, quoting with approval 'a wine expert in conversation with a *Morning Post* representative yesterday', and the same man's chapter on champagne in his *The Wines of France*, published in 1924, after he had visited Champagne a number of times, and learned something about wine:

> The people responsible for the present riots [he wrote in 1911, quoting the 'wine expert' before going on to his own pontifications] were the peasant vignerons who sold wine to the makers of champagne. These makers were rarely themselves vignerons, but bought their supplies of raw wine from the peasants, blended them, and made them up into champagne. In a special brand there might be wine from fifteen different vineyards. The actual winegrowers were now agitating to prevent wines from the Loire being brought into the Champagne district to be made up into champagne. They had no wines of their own to sell owing to the failure of the vintage, and yet wished to prevent the industry of champagne-making from being kept going with suitable wines from other districts. Success in this would be harmful to themselves. The industry would be paralysed, and very many people engaged in making and handling champagne would be thrown out of work. Some of the labour engaged in the industry is very highly paid, that, for instance, of the skilful workers who shake the bottles from time to time—a necessary part of the particular process of secondary fermentation which is responsible for sparkling wine. A very delicate hand is needed for this shaking, and the work consequently is rewarded with high wages. If rioting succeeds in stopping the industry these and other workers will be the chief sufferers.
>
> In ordinary times the Champagne district can supply, or nearly supply, the demand of the champagne makers, taking a French and not an English definition of champagne. Now it cannot. But the peasants seem possessed with an idea that there will be a remedy for bad seasons in declaring that since champagne cannot be made with the wine they have not got it shall

not be made with any other. It is typical of the craze that afflicts so many of the French now for legislation. To have a law passed is their remedy for everything, even for rainy seasons. The delimitation demanded to prevent Loire wine coming into the Champagne country would do no good at all: yet the craze for it is the origin of these destructive riots.

Could anything be more obtuse? But in 1924 he wrote:

As soon as the news reached Paris, I hurried down to Epernay, which was the centre of the trouble. Even in the spring sunshine it was a depressing excursion, and at the time there seemed neither rhyme nor reason to excuse the melancholy sight of gutted houses, smashed bottles, and burnt and trampled vines, though events have shown that the destruction was not so senseless as it appeared at first. It was doubtless regrettable that the vignerons should have had recourse to direct action, to use the phrase current in those days of revolutionary Syndicalism, but it is satisfactory to know that they attained their object, which was the interest of every Champagne drinker, and it is hard to see how they could have attained it by constitutional means. The Champenois regarded without much surprise or horror the burning of houses and the sacking of cellars, so long as they were not personally concerned: the more bottles of outside wines masquerading as Champagne destroyed, the better they were pleased. Most of the damage was done at Ay, where a whole row of buildings, the warehouses and cellars of various merchants, was absolutely gutted, and over that dismal spectacle not a vigneron would shed a tear. He was content to point to the premises of one or two firms, which had suffered no harm, and would explain that those who made their Champagne only from Champagne grapes had suffered no injury at all. Exasperation was natural enough, for as soon as there seemed a prospect of the existing situation being changed, enormous quantities of cheap wines were poured into the district, to be transformed into Champagne, before any new law could come into force.

There was one thing, however, about the riots that did astonish many Champenois. The vigneron has an affection and respect for the vines on which his livelihood depends that are almost religious in their intensity: he would as soon strike a baby as trample a young vine shoot under foot. But on this occasion not only were tender shoots and 'sweet buds', just beginning, 'like flocks, to feed in air', trampled mercilessly under foot, but hundreds of precious vines were deliberately destroyed. Thus in one of the finest vineyards between Ay and Dizy, belonging to a very well-known Epernay firm, almost all the black *pinot* plants were burnt. To protect them from the frost, they had been covered with a little thatch of straw, which ran the whole length of the rows, and the rioters had amused themselves by setting fire to it at different places, until the whole vineyard was ruined—a mere black patch across the chalk. It was this pitiless slaughter of the unborn grape, this unnatural cruelty to the vine, which persuaded many of the Champenois that the worst part of destruction was done, not by their own people, but by agitators and professional bullies of the General Confederation of Labour, sent down from Paris to inflame the trouble. Be that as it may, good came out of evil, and the result of the riots has been that both vigneron and consumer have legal guarantees as to the authenticity of all sparkling Champagne sold in France.

Severe though the authorities were with the rioters, the government was sympathetic over their grievances, as indeed it had been all along—sensitive, at any rate, to the wine-growers' lobby. A new draft bill was hurried through in less than two months from the day of the Ay outbreak. Its recognition of two distinct zones for champagne—one confined almost entirely to the classic region of the Marne, and a much smaller *deuxième zone* for the Aube—was obviously unworkable, but the bill was still being debated when war broke out three years later, and this particular clause was eventually dropped.

But although the three years until the outbreak of war were spent in discussion, and then the war itself held everything up, the government had shown willing, and on the whole the vignerons in general were satisfied that something would be done.

Now, by a succession of laws dating from 1919, the champagne area is strictly delimited. It includes parts of the Aisne and the Aube, but these are too small and unimportant for the growers of the Marne to be resentful. Most important, there are stringently drawn safeguards against the fraudulent use of wine from other areas, and a Comité Interprofessionel du Vin de Champagne to see that all regulations are strictly observed: even unfermented champagne must not be moved from one parish to another of the region without an official permit.

Through its constituent commissions, every branch of the trade and every ancillary is represented on the Comité, from grower of grape to maker of wine, and from the makers of bottles and makers of corks to the firms that draw the wire that holds the cork to the bottle. The state is represented, and the money needed to support the Comité figures in France's annual budget: it is raised from taxes on grapes grown and on bottles sold.

Basically, this quite remarkably powerful body exists to protect grower and maker[6] but obviously it protects the consumer, too: it ensures a fair price to the vigneron for his grapes and makes quite impossible the sharp practices that led to the outbreaks of 1911. In 1960, with the second of two cases in the British courts against the shippers of the Spanish 'Perelada', it successfully protected the name 'champagne' from the makers elsewhere of other sparkling wines.

Ask any *champenois*, grower or maker, and he will tell you that all the protective legislation from 1919 to 1941, with the creation of the Comité Interprofessionel to make it effective, is due solely and entirely to the rioters of 1911.

It is time, indeed, that alongside the statue of Dom Pérignon at Hautvillers there was one of a sturdy knave with a bludgeon.

[6] Patrick Forbes, op. cit., pp. 223–31.

6. Bubble and Bottle

Bollinger is, and always has been, an Ay house, and Ay is the centre of all its activities. But the grapes from which it makes its champagne do not all come from the vineyards of the Vallée de la Marne, of which Ay is, as it were, the capital town. Although the wine of Ay is the only one 'that unblended gives a more or less satisfactory champagne in the modern acceptation of the term',[1] Bollinger would still not be the completely balanced wine that it is, if they did. The best champagne is a balanced wine because it is a blended wine.

So the grapes for Bollinger champagne come not only from the Ay vineyards, some of which—including many that are Bollinger's own—sweep right up to the walls of the firm's main building there, and almost to those of Madame Bollinger's house and those of her fellow directors. Others are grown elsewhere, whether in Bollinger's own vineyards or in those of other, smaller, growers who sell to Bollinger—black grapes, as from the Ay vineyards themselves, from the Montagne de Reims; white from the Côte des Blancs.

[1] See chapter I.

So, in addition to the main press-house at Ay—just across the narrow Rue Jules-Lobet from Madame Bollinger's house—with its two great wooden presses, each capable of taking 5,200 kilograms of grapes instead of the customary 4,000, there are smaller Bollinger *vendangeoirs*—press-houses—at Verzenay and at Louvois, in the Montagne de Reims, some ten and seven miles, respectively, north-east of Ay, and at Cuis, five miles south, on the other side of the Marne, in the Côte des Blancs.

It is interesting not only to note that these three press-houses are set strategically close to Bollinger-owned vineyards, but to recall that the de Villermont family, from which the firm descends, owned vineyards in two of these three places—in Cuis and in Verzenay—as long ago as the beginning of the eighteenth century.

There are eight Bollinger presses in these four press-houses and, in addition, the firm rents presses in other villages at vintage time.

With the exception of the two 5,200-kilogram presses at Ay, each press will take 4,000 kilograms of grapes. It is laid down by the strict laws that govern the making and the naming of champagne that no more than the first 100 litres of juice from each 150 kilograms of grapes is entitled to the *appellation*; so from each 4,000-kilogram vat only the first 2,666 litres of juice can be used for champagne. (And so, in proportion, with the 5,200-kilogram vats of Ay.)

The champagne cask, which when empty is called *un fut*, holds 200 litres when full, and then becomes *une pièce*. So that, as near as may be, each press will produce thirteen casks of juice entitled, when it has fermented into wine, to the name 'champagne'. But not to the name 'Bollinger'.

The first 2,000 litres—the juice, that is, that fills the first ten casks of the thirteen—is the best: the *vin de cuvée*, all of which goes to make Bollinger. The remaining three casks are the *vin de taille*.

This *vin de taille* is divided by quality into two. The first two casks of juice (usually referred to at this point as *moût*, or 'must') constitute the *premier taille* which, slightly coarsened though it is by a certain amount of what is pressed from stalks and pips, has more fruit and is less acid than the *vin de cuvée*, and this 410 litres, or some of it, may well be needed in some light years to augment its character and body.

The *deuxième taille*, though it is still entitled to the *appellation* of champagne, is never used in Bollinger. Some of this 205 litres from each press is sold to lesser houses (for it makes a tolerable champagne) to be made into cheaper brands or into B.O.B. champagnes, which is to say champagnes that are sold under the name and label of firms other than the makers: 'buyer's own brand'.

Some juice—pinkish, thin and sharp—could still be squeezed by a more powerful press from the solidly concentrated cake of skin, pips and stalks now remaining. In the old days, this used to be done and, with the addition of water, a wine made, known as *vin de sucre*. It is now forbidden to make this, and Bollinger sell their solid residue to be distilled elsewhere into the strong, earthy, colourless spirit of the region: *eau-de-vie de marc*, or *marc de Champagne*.[2]

The must runs from the press into a concrete *belon*, and straight from there into a glass-lined *cuve de debourbage*, or decanting vat, where it remains for eight to twelve hours during which, helped by a small addition of sulphur dioxide, the stalks, pips, fragments of soil, and even sometimes scraps of wire from the vines fall to the bottom.

From here, the juice is run straight into 200-litre wooden casks —if at one of the press-houses outside Ay, into the same casks in which it will be transported to the Ay cellars, for although some firms now carry their must in metal road-tankers, Bollinger believes in wood. The casks are sealed for the journey, but there is a small escape-vent by the bung, with a straw inserted, lest fermentation begin early, while the must is on the road.

Normally, though, the juice is still juice, not wine. It will become wine when it ferments fully, and at Bollinger the first fermentation is, as it always used to be, in wood. (What gives champagne its sparkle is the second fermentation, in bottle.) Many other great houses now use steel and concrete vats lined

---

[2] A good *marc de Champagne*, though not to everyone's taste, is usually regarded as more delicate than a *marc de Bourgogne*. Goyard is a good firm.

with glass or even, in a very few still more up-to-date instances, with a synthetic resin lining.[3]

As I have already observed, though, Bollinger believe that there is nothing like wood—that it permits the young wine to 'breathe', as steel and concrete and glass and synthetic resins cannot possibly do, and also that fermentation in 200-litre casks as compared with the enormous vats is easier to watch and to control. But it is much more expensive. There is a certain amount of loss of wine through seepage and overflow, as there is not from the impermeable vats, and a litre of wine spilled means a loss of five francs, which is nearly eight shillings; there has to be more handling, more cleaning, and more repairing, all of which is reflected in higher labour costs per bottle at Bollinger than elsewhere.

The casks are made of oak from the forests of the Argonne, a hundred miles away to the east. The staves are shaped by axe, with the grain, not by saw, against it, lest the wood 'bleed'; the new casks are fumigated with brimstone, checked as being water-tight, and then 'broken in' with the cheap *taille* before being used for the *cuvée*.

There is a cooperage at Bollinger, forming one side of the courtyard of Madame Bollinger's house, which at one time was used for making casks, but it is used now only for repairs: nowadays, the casks are made where the oak is grown.

*   *   *

On the Sunday nearest to St John's Day (24 June), as John is the patron saint of the coopers, it used to be the custom in Ay to hold a *course aux tonneaux*—a cask race—between the various champagne houses.

It is significant that nowadays there is no firm in Ay with enough experience in handling casks to compete against Bollinger, so that for some years now the race has been a purely internal Bollinger affair, in which a dozen or thereabouts of the

[3] There is a telling contrast in the two photographs facing p. 257 of Mr Patrick Forbes's *Champagne*: 'casks for the first fermentation' and 'vats for the first fermentation'. The old-fashioned, wooden casks shown are, in fact, Bollinger's; the vats are typical of a big, new-fashioned firm.

firm's cellarmen race their casks along the straightest street in Ay—taking pride in using only the tip of the forefinger to propel the casks and to keep the wobbly brutes on a straight course— for a silver cup presented by Madame.

I have been told that a similar race still takes place in Reims, but that none of the houses there will take up the repeated Bollinger challenge.

* * *

In Champagne, an underground cellar is *une cave*; *un cellier* is an above-ground shed or store-room such as in Spain is called a *bodega* and in Bordeaux *un chai*—a word not used in Champagne.

By Champagne standards, the Bollinger *caves* are modest indeed—a mere three miles of galleries cut into the chalk, compared with the fantastic seventeen miles or so of Moët et Chandon, and the vast galleries of Mercier, served by an electric train.

They include, though, the original cellars of the Comte de Villermont, the first Jacques Bollinger's father-in-law, as well as those of the old house of Duminy, next door, which Bollinger bought in 1937, and have since extended.

And the modest three miles of cellarage holds no fewer than five and a half million bottles of champagne (or their equivalent: some are magnums, some double-magnums, some halves, some pints)—between four and five years' supplies of Bollinger. Employed there, and in the above-ground *celliers*, are some eighty to a hundred workers, who do a forty-hour week, get a free ration of champagne, and do not allow the strong communist tradition of their craft to conflict with an intense loyalty to the house of Bollinger and an equally intense pride in its wine.

'His politics are as red as his face', one of the directors said amiably of a sturdy, rubicund cellar-hand, with whom he had just exchanged the heartiest of greetings. I remembered that it was in much the same way that one of the Moët directors had grinned at me when, on Mr Khrushchev's visit to their cellars in 1960, half the population of Epernay had produced little red flags to wave at their then hero.

Cellar-workers are left-wing by blood, like British dockers

and coal-miners: like them, too, they form an aristocracy of labour. It is different in the vineyards, where vignerons, also proudly skilled craftsmen, are usually peasant-proprietors, and enormously more conservative.

*   *   *

It is to a first-floor *cellier* that the casks are taken for the *bouillage*—the first, violent fermentation of the must, which begins about ten days after the vintage and lasts for about a fortnight. To begin with, each cask has about 8 per cent of its content drawn off into others to leave space for the first angry bubbling, and lessen the chance of loss through overflow. Then, as the most turbulent stage of the process subsides, the casks are topped up again—to prevent oxidization by the outside air—and left to a gentler fermentation that will last for another couple of weeks or rather more, so that the whole process of first fermentation will have taken some six or seven weeks from the time that the grapes are gathered. The casks are not sealed until fermentation is complete, lest pressure build up that would burst them.

Another three weeks of rest for what has now become wine— a fully fermented, dry, still wine—and it is now the end of the year, and cold. Remember that the casks are in an above-ground *cellier*, not below ground in a *cave*, so that their temperature depends on that of the outside air. The colder it is now the better: doors and windows of the *cellier* are flung open to let in the winter chill, so that any last flicker, as it were, of fermentation shall be brought to a halt, and so that residual impurities shall fall to the bottom of the casks.[4]

Once the young wine from each cask has been tasted, this is the time for the *premier soutirage*—the first racking, when the clear wine is taken from off its lees, by being drawn from one wooden cask to another. This, at any rate, is how it is done at Bollinger, where they will have no truck either with a vat-to-vat

[4] Since this was written, Bollinger have installed an air-conditioning plant in the *cellier*, to provide more precise control of temperature for this enormously important period of weeks. The firm is by no means averse to innovations, but will not countenance innovations merely for the sake of economies.

racking, or with filtration, which some houses believe in as a quick and economical method of racking, but which Bollinger regard as tending to rob so delicate a wine of some of its nature.

Within a couple of weeks, round about the end of January and beginning of February, the time comes for a second similar, tasting and then racking, and this is the time, too, when the various casks of each district and quality are all blended together, but still in their respective groups. In other words, if there are (say) a hundred casks of *vin de cuvée* from various Ay vineyards, they are all mixed together—only at this point, and briefly, are vats used at all, as mixing vessels—and redistributed into a hundred other casks, so that a homogeneous blend of Ay *vin de cuvée* is now assembled into a group of casks, the wine in which is all of the one quality. So, too, with any casks there may be of Ay *vin de taille*. So with the wine of Cuis, of Verzenay, of Louvois and of Bouzy.

It is cold in Champagne now, in January and February, and the wine rests, while such solids as still remain after the two rackings settle slowly to the bottoms of the casks.

*   *   *

Meanwhile, in the clinically austere little white-tiled tasting-room, away from the cellar's smells of young wine and old damp, of chalk and wood and brick, there is going on what Mr Patrick Forbes has described as, 'the most difficult and the most distinctive phase of the entire *méthode champenoise*: the selection of the still wines that are to compose [the champagne-maker's] blends. The selection is called the preparation of the *cuvée*.'

If it has been a good enough year for a vintage wine to be made, there is blending to be done, nevertheless. Perhaps the Pinot Noir has been a disappointment in one vineyard, a success in another; perhaps the Chardonnay is lacking a little in fragrance; how is the balance struck? Perhaps the year has been 'big', in which case, after many repeated tastings of the wine from every vineyard represented, it will be decided to use rather more than the usual 30 per cent or so of white grapes, rather less than the 70 or so of black. I well remember Madame Bollinger saying in London, in 1964, when the 1959 was launched, that the danger had been of producing a soft, flabby wine, lacking in crispness and delicacy: much more white grapes were used than usual.

Not every year in Champagne is a vintage year, though, but every year a wine must be made. Even at Bollinger (where 39 per cent of the total production, averaged over a period of years, is vintage wine, compared with 20 per cent for the champagne trade as a whole) non-vintage is the heart of the matter, and the backbone of the business.

In a year that is not itself going to be a vintage year—and I have the year 1968 very much in mind, for I saw a good deal in 1969 of the trouble that Bollinger went to in order to make the best use of what was far from being, or ever becoming, a great wine— the answer is to blend, not with greater care than usual, for that, I think, would hardly be possible, but to draw upon a greater range of older and fuller-flavoured wines than would normally be necessary, or even, in a really good year, advisable, to give style and character and staying-power to the wine of a light year.

Beginning in February, and going on until the end of March, or the beginning of April, there are two or three tastings a week, for five or six weeks, of the reserves that have been kept in magnums for eventual blending of unblended, still wines from possibly as many as eighteen different districts of the region and of various vintages between 1928 and 1964. (This was the number of districts and range of vintage years tasted in 1969—more than a hundred in all: eighteen districts multiplied by at least half a dozen different years.)

After a poorish, lightish year, such as 1968, most of these were the wines of 'big' years: this is where the self-sacrifice of a firm such as Bollinger comes in, for in every good year it puts away reserves of still wine that could far more profitably be made into vintage wine. Indeed, it always puts away, in a great year, the very best wines of all.

In a poor year, some of the best of what may in its own right be only an indifferent wine is just as carefully put away—its very thinness may well be immensely useful in a very 'big' year to add lightness to what might otherwise be a heavy flaccid wine.

There is a slight *pétillance*—a sort of very subdued sparkle—in the wine in these magnums because, as the second fermentation has not been induced in them, as it is in bottle when champagne is being made, the first fermentation has never quite fulfilled itself. This very slight 'prickle' in the wine keeps it in good condition: it would be lost if the reserves were all kept in vats, as they are at all other champagne houses now save Bollinger and perhaps, at most, one or two others. It is cheaper and easier to keep reserves in trouble-free vats but, they say at Bollinger, the better condition of the wine kept in magnums justifies the extra expense and inconvenience.

At Bollinger, there is a committee of five, consisting of Madame Bollinger herself—at the time of writing, more than seventy years old, and with nearly fifty years of experience—with M. Claude d'Hautefeuille, her deputy as chairman; M. Yves Moret de Rocheprise, who is in charge of the vineyards; and M. Christian Bizot, in charge of sales. All these are directors; all, one way or another, are related. The fifth is M. Guy Adam, the *chef de cave*, son-in-law and pupil of M. Bergeot, who died in 1968—having held the same high office for more than fifty years, still a living legend for his dedication to Bollinger, both family and wine.

As Mr Patrick Forbes has observed, 'what makes an outstanding *chef de cave* is not a diploma but a good pair of eyes, a nose and a palate capable of detecting and defining the minutest nuances of smell and taste, an amazing memory, and long experience, experience both gained in his own lifetime and transmitted to him in his blood by his Champenois forebears. For in the final analysis the art of blending depends not on chemical or mathematical formulae, but on gift and flair.'

True, but although M. Guy Adam, the *chef de cave* at Bollinger, has all the gifts enumerated here, there is no doubt who is chairman of the Bollinger tasting committee. Madame Bollinger leans her bicycle against the wall outside; divests herself, if the weather is inclement, of a layer of assorted oilskins, and enters the tasting-room, to take her place, half sitting, half leaning, against an old-fashioned radiator (which I do not think ever works) hard by the sink where the glasses are rinsed.

Not at first meeting, because then she smiles, and her smile is radiant, but at first sight, before one is introduced, one might say that Madame Bollinger's face is expressionless—even dour, as befits her Scottish ancestry. When she speaks to a friend or a guest, or when she is surrounded by her great-nephews and great-nieces, it becomes not what the Scots, but what the French, mean by *douce*: to the Scots this means 'sedate', or 'demure'; to the French it means 'sweet' or 'winning'. In the tasting-room it becomes engagingly expressive: the quiet, dignified, customarily expressionless features of a Scottish or of a *tourangelle* gentle-woman manage to convey, with a cock of the eyebrow and a pursing of the lips, that this Avize 1928, that Bouzy 1964, will or will not do for the finished *cuvée*—and it is Madame's cock of the eyebrow or pursing of the lips that the others watch. I do not say that no one would disagree, but he would taste again, to be quite sure of his own mind, before he spoke it, for experience has shown that Madame usually knows best. Not merely that this wine or that is better than one or another, but how it will develop over the years, which is a much more important thing to decide—and much more difficult.

That, too, is a matter of experience. The average age of the committee of five is in the middle fifties, and there is an aggregate of about a century of tasting. But Madame Bollinger has the advantage of some fifteen years' start over each of a couple of her colleagues, and getting on for thirty each over the other two.

And with champagne, more than with any other wine, as I have discovered for myself in the Bollinger and in other tasting-rooms in the region, experience counts. It is harder to compare a number of different champagnes than it is to compare clarets, say, or ports—almost as hard as to compare brandies or whiskies. The coolness at which the wines must be drunk, the acidity, the sparkle—all combine, after more than a very few have been tasted, to numb the palate and to cloud the judgement.

Once a short list of two or three potential blends has been decided on, these also are tasted, probably two or three times a week, for about a month, because the blends are constantly changing in bottle, until a final decision is made on a wine that is not only good in itself but also consistent with the traditional Bollinger 'style'.

These tastings that constitute the preparation of the *cuvée* are by no means the only ones. The tasting panel meets twice a week for virtually all the other forty-five or so weeks of the year.

Sometimes, it is to taste sample bottles of the vintage or the non-vintage Bollinger currently on sale; sometimes, to taste the vintage against a representative range of competitors of the same year, or the non-vintage against competitors' non-vintage wines available at the same shop at the same time. (Bottles both of Bollinger and of the other wines are bought from Fauchon, that *de luxe* grocers-cum-wine merchants by the Madeleine in Paris— a sort of apotheosized Fortnums—for it can be assumed that here the bottles will have been well-kept, and that stocks of non-vintage wines are frequently turned over.)

Sometimes, a range of the premium qualities, or 'fancy bottles', is tasted alongside Bollinger's similarly expensive R.D.,[5] and again it is amusing to watch Madame Bollinger's shrug of the shoulders to indicate that this or that much-puffed fancy bottle is lacking in character, or the wry smile and the approving nod that acknowledges that a near and respected rival is well into the Bollinger class.

*   *   *

After the second racking, the January–February resting of the wine, and the blending—again, at Bollinger, this is effected in wooden casks—there is a three-week process of fining by isinglass, which sinks slowly through the wine, taking the last impurities with it, as the egg-whites do that are used in the claret country. Then a third and final racking in cask and now, in the spring, about eight or nine months after the vintage, the wine is at last ready for bottling, and for its transformation from a still to a sparkling wine.

The clear wine is drawn from the fined casks to spend one night in a vat before being bottled, and it is in this vat that the sugar and yeasts are added that will encourage and reinforce the natural tendency of the wine of the region to ferment a second time in the spring after the vintage.

The yeasts are cultivated grape yeasts; the sugar is not a sweetening agent but will be completely consumed, turned by

[5] See chapter 8.

the yeasts, when the wine is in bottle, into alcohol and carbonic acid gas—the gas that, firmly imprisoned, gives champagne its bubble. The addition of the sugar at this stage (it is dissolved in a small amount of the same wine to which it will be added, and is called the *liqueur de tirage*) is not to be confused with the *liqueur d'expédition* which, as we shall see later, is added at the very end of the champagne process, after the disgorgement, and determines the degree of the wine's dryness or sweetness.

Within a matter of hours the wine is in bottle: at Bollinger, where they bottle the equivalent of something like a million bottles a year, about one-sixth of the total goes into magnums—double bottles—about another one-sixth into half-bottles, and almost all the remaining two-thirds into the standard 78-centilitre bottle, except for one two-hundred-and-fiftieth of the total, which goes into a thousand jeroboams or double-magnums.

These are the bottles in which fermentation takes place, and the bottles that will eventually reach the consumer. So far as I know, Bollinger is the only firm that ferments in jeroboams as well as in magnums, bottles, imperial pints, and half-bottles—other houses ferment only in magnums, bottles and halves[6] and have to *decant* from bottles to produce jeroboams and, sometimes, even bigger bottles—methusalehs, nebuchadnezzars, and the like—for special orders, just as they do for quarter-bottles.

Fermenting in double-magnums is a risky business, which is why no other firm that I know of will tackle it: if one is broken in the cellar, or spoiled by a bad cork (which is a loss the maker has to stand, wherever the corkiness is detected, at a private house or a restaurant), the damage is four times that of a bottle broken or 'corked'. Bollinger run the risk a thousand times a year because they believe, that there is a demand for double-magnums as special presents or for special parties; that the bigger the bottle the better the wine, so that the purchaser of a double-magnum really is getting marginally better Bollinger than if he bought four bottles; but that this does not apply if the wine has

[6] Some, too, bless them, but all too few, these days, in imperial pints—half-way between bottles and halves. An ideal size for two at luncheon and for one at dinner: Bollinger bottle some 3,000 a year, and I wish more restaurants listed them.

been decanted—instead, then, of being slightly better than a bottle, it will be slightly inferior, for however skilfully champagne is decanted from one bottle to another, it inevitably loses a little of its sparkle and a little of its bouquet, and will not keep for so long in such good condition.

At this same point in the process, we come across another Bollinger singularity.

Although the wine is now in the bottles that will eventually reach the consumer, the bottles are not yet wearing the corks that their purchasers will pop. For before the champagne is ready for drinking it must be rid of its sediment, and this will require that eventually one cork is removed and another takes its place. The first cork is the *bouchon de tirage*, and virtually all the champagne houses now use crown-corks for their non-vintage wines, most of them even for their vintage.

One can tell from the bottle, at one's own or at a restaurant table, which has been used. The bottle that was crown-corked until it was freed of its sediment, and then re-corked, will have a *bague couronne*—a crown ring—like this:

whereas the bottle that had the old-fashioned *bouchon de tirage*— the same size and shape as the second and final cork—will have a *bague carré*, or square ring, like this:

 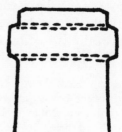

There is no mistaking which has been used, though sometimes one can jump to the wrong conclusion about the general practice of a particular firm: I was once sharing with a friend in the champagne trade a bottle of a well-known, much advertised brand with a very big sale. To my surprise, I found the wine being poured from a bottle with a *bague carré*. 'But I thought that they, of all people, used crown-corks,' I said.

'So they do,' said my friend: 'but they also buy wine in bottle from some of the *manipulants*.[7] They buy it before disgorgement; disgorge it themselves; and then dress it up with their own labels and their own branded second corks. But a lot of the smaller *manipulants* still use the old-fashioned *bouchon de tirage*. What this *bague carré* tells us is that this wine wasn't made by the people whose label is on it: not bad, though, is it?'

Nor was it—better, perhaps, than it would have been if it had been made by the people who claimed to have done so.

Generally, I am told, 95 per cent of the bottles sold to the champagne trade as a whole are of the crown-cork type, only 5 per cent of the *bague carré*. Over the whole trade, some 15 per cent of total production is vintage wine, 85 per cent non-vintage (Bollinger's is 38 per cent vintage, 62 non-vintage). So this is a fair indication that pretty well all non-vintage wine, now, and even some vintage must be crown-corked to begin with.

There is a case for the crown-cork. For one thing, not only can the first corking be done entirely by machine, but so can the later removal of cork and sediment, whereas the old-fashioned first cork has to be fed by hand into a similarly old-fashioned machine so that it goes in undamaged and the right way up. So, too, with its removal: a machine can remove the crown-cork, whereas the *agrafe*—the heavy metal clip that secures the old type of cork—has to be removed by hand.

The crown-cork is, of course, lined with a layer of cork or plastic, so that there is no metal in contact with the wine, but the layer is so thin that, even if of cork, there is no danger of its becoming diseased and the wine's becoming 'corked'—its taste and smell affected. (The risk is rare indeed even with the old type.)

[7] See page 45.

Most important, the whole operation is much cheaper, both because of the saving in labour costs, and the relative prices of cork and crown-cork, and nothing is lost, say the modernists, in quality.

This may well be so. Conclusive proof, one way or the other, would be difficult and expensive to produce. Certainly, I have enjoyed many a delicious glass of wine from bottles bearing the labels of distinguished houses and with *bagues couronnes*, and I would not care to say that the wine would have been one whit the finer if it had originally been corked rather than crown-corked.

Bollinger, though, experimented with crown-corks in 1961, and decided then to stick to the old-fashioned way. A proper cork, says Madame Bollinger, 'lets the wine breathe', whereas under a crown-cork, she decided, too much acidity was left in the wine. It may be that it is her temperament rather than her taste that tells her so—that Bollinger is as good as it is not because of the old-fashioned first cork but because of the care that goes into all the other stages of the wine-making process, and because of the quality of the grapes. Perhaps even because of the attitude of mind that prompts the firm to choose almost instinctively the older-fashioned rather than the newer-fangled way. But if it does have even the most marginally minute effect on the quality of the wine it can only be for the better, and the decision is typically Bollinger.

*   *   *

Nine months have gone by, but there is a longer gestation yet. In single file, the bottles march by conveyor-belt from above-ground *cellier* to below-ground *cave*. The heavy metal *agrafe* is cut deep into the top of the cork, which is sharply divided at the top, so that the bottles look like grenadiers of the Seven Years' War, in their tall, mitred caps. They are bound for a long stay in the cool and the dark.

So far as the law is concerned a non-vintage champagne could be in the hands of the consumer in only one year after being bottled. Most champagne shippers feel that this is too short a time: the average over the trade as a whole for non-vintage wine is two to two and a half years—for Bollinger it is four and a half.

IX   Nearly half a century's experience: Madame Bollinger in the tasting room.

X *Remuage*: By rotating and oscillating the bottles daily over many months a skilled *remueur*, here at work on jeroboams—double magnums, causes the sediment to be precipitated on to the cork before disgorgement. With ordinary bottles the *remueur* handles two at a time.

XI   Madame Bollinger, born 1899, makes her daily vineyard inspection.

XII Madame Bollinger returning home.

For vintage wine, the law says three years, but Bollinger leaves it for five in the *cave* before it is launched on the market, which means that, as the vintage does not all leave the *cave* at once, the last bottles of a particular vintage to reach the consumer before it is replaced by the next vintage will have had seven years in the Bollinger cellars. Thus, the 1964 vintage Bollinger was launched in October 1969, precisely five years after the grapes had been gathered, but it will not be replaced until the latter part of 1971.

For all but a few months of this period they are left undisturbed, binned flat. Some firms at this point put an extra china-clay fining in the bottles, to help the sediment to form more quickly, so that this binning period can be shortened—the shorter the time wine is waiting to be sold, the shorter the time capital is tied up—but Bollinger do not. What they do instead, in common with some other of the older-fashioned houses, is to have all the bottles shaken after six months—sometimes once more—to move the residual sugar about and so make sure that fermentation is complete. This is the *changement de place*.

*   *   *

With some champagnes, the second fermentation may take no longer than a week, but at Bollinger, because of the richness of the grapes, and the consequent relatively high alcoholic content of the wine, which means more work for the yeasts to do, it takes about three months. The process is deliberately prolonged, too, by the bottles' being kept in the coolest part of the cellar. In almost all the processes that go to make champagne, the slower the better, but a close watch is kept on the progress of the fermentation—sample bottles are opened so that the residual sugar can be measured, and the pressure of gas is checked by means of a syringe-like gauge inserted through the cork—and if it is too slow in making a start, then bottles may be moved to a less cold corner.

Whether there is any clearly understood chemical reason, I do not know, but the slower the fermentation the more certain it is that the bubble in the bottle at the completion of the process will be light, or small, and 'busy'—or perhaps 'continuous' is the word. We all know the kind of sparkling wine that makes a lot of fuss on being poured out, with a big bubble in the glass that subsides almost immediately—braggart wines. It is a matter of pride to a good champagne house that the wine in the glass should go on sparkling in the glass long after it was poured, fulfilling the promise that it made when the bottle was opened.

So, too, just as a slow fermentation means the right kind of bubble, so does the subsequent prolonged period of rest mean mellowness, balance, flavour and bouquet. This is why, as has already been observed, Bollinger mature their non-vintage wine for four and a half years after the vintage, as against the customary two and a half, and the legal minimum of one, and their vintage for at least five. (The premium quality Bollinger R.D., as we shall see in a later chapter, enjoys a longer period still.)

Throughout this long period, a fine sediment in the bottle is forming, composed of exhausted yeast cells and solids from the wine, and another reason for the long period of maturing after fermentation is that the longer the wine remains on its sediment, the fuller the flavour.

But the sediment must eventually be removed before the wine can be shipped, and for this to be done the sediment has to be shifted from the side of the bottle where, as the bottle has been horizontal for so long, it has now settled.

Two processes are involved: *remuage*, or riddling, and *dégorgement*—disgorgement.

Bollinger tried a *remuage* machine over a period of months in 1964 and decided to stick to the traditional method of *remuage* by hand, in spite of the considerably greater cost in skilled labour, for the machine will do in three weeks, under one machine-minder, what it takes a number of skilled workers as many months to do by hand. But do much better, say Bollinger.

About a year before shipment, the bottles are placed, neck downwards up to the shoulder, in racks, called *pupitres*, standing in inverted Vs, so slotted that each bottle can be placed pointing downwards at an angle, and the slots so bevelled that the angle of the bottles can be changed from almost completely horizontal to almost completely vertical. First, they are left for three weeks, to let the sediment drop, and then they are thus changed, over the weeks, for some three to five months, by *remueurs*, the most highly-skilled and the highest-paid workers in the cellars, who rotate, oscillate and tilt, rotate, oscillate and tilt each bottle by incredibly quick movements of their huge, yet precisely accurate hands—hands so accurately controlled, indeed, as to be able to move each bottle an eighth of a turn, no more, no less, with each movement. Those firms that use china-clay (see page 103) cannot afford to have the bottles oscillated—only gently shaken, lest the china-clay permeate the wine. Here again Bollinger benefit from their refusal to take short cuts.

A skilled *remueur* can rotate 40,000 bottles, and oscillate 20,000 of them, in a working day, his hands flickering at a fantastic rate over the *pupitre* and, as each bottle is rotated, at an eighth of a turn at a time, through a number of circles, being simultaneously shaken, and its angle of tilt increased, it eventually is almost vertical, cork downwards, with the sediment now adhering to the bottom of the cork, and the wine perfectly clear.

This makes disgorgement possible.

But before the disgorgement takes place, Bollinger reap the benefit of their old-fashioned insistence on a proper cork instead of a crown-cork as the *bouchon de tirage*. For the old-fashioned cork means that the bottle can be left for longer in its upside-down position than it could on a crown-cork, the wine still deriving fullness and flavour from the sediment.

Eventually, though, the sediment must be got rid of. This is briskly effected by artificially freezing the neck of the bottle, thus solidifying the sediment, which flies out as a virtually solid piece of sand-coloured stone when the *dégorgeur*—the next most highly-paid cellar-worker after the *remueur*—snips the *agrafe* and releases the cork. The *dégorgeur* holds the bottle against the light; sniffs; and leaves the bottle underneath a spring-loaded temporary cork to keep in the gas until the next operation.

But between popping the cork and putting his thumb over the bottle after the sediment has been discharged, he has deliberately allowed a little of the froth to escape—partly to carry with it any loose specks of sediment still clinging to the inside of the neck of the bottle, partly to increase very slightly the space left by the discharge of the sediment and of the minute amount of frozen wine immediately below it.

For this space has to be refilled, and the character and style of a particular brand of champagne depends very largely on how this is done. Partly, the bottle is topped up with some of the same wine as that already in the bottle: this is the *remplissage*. Partly, there is the allied process of *dosage*, or liqueuring—the adding of a further amount of the same wine in which has been dissolved some cane sugar. This mixture is the *liqueur d'expédition*, and it determines how sweet or how dry the particular champagne will be.

All champagne is dry by nature, and much the more so because it has been fermented not once, but twice, so that all residual sugar is consumed by yeasts.

In the very best champagnes, what the *dosage* does is ever so slightly to soften the austerity of perfect dryness, leaving the wine still crisply and refreshingly dry, but not astringently so. It can also be the means of deliberately making the champagne into a sweet wine, for there are those (such as Russian grand dukes in the old days and, today, South American tycoons and some Oriental potentates) who always prefer their champagne to be sweet; others who enjoy (as I do) a glass of sweet champagne with a peach or a pear after one of those infrequent champagne dinners—which, to my mind, should be preceded by a dry non-vintage wine, accompanied by a fuller, but still dry, vintage, and end with sweet.

(Not that I am so fond as my *champenois* friends are of champagne as a wine for all courses, nor do many of them ever serve sweet champagne at all: it is the custom of the country to serve old, dry champagne with fruit and puddings, which is not to my taste or, I think, to that of most Englishmen.)

Another service that liqueuring can perform, if it is pretty generous, though not yet enough to make the wine truly sweet, is to mask the inadequacies of a thin wine, made perhaps from the cheapest grapes or from as many pressings as are legally permitted, or from both. '*Dosage*', says M. Christian Bizot, 'can cover a multitude of sins.'

And over all, of course, it is one of the factors, along with the choice of grapes, the blending of black grapes and white grapes and of this vineyard and that and, in non-vintage wines, of the wines of different years, that determine the house 'style' of a champagne. Amongst the very best dozen or so champagnes, some are drier than others, some sweeter; some are lighter, some are fuller-flavoured. And those that are sweeter are not necessarily *sweet*—it makes more sense to say that they are marginally less dry than others. The very good Lanson Black Label, for instance, is just such a non-vintage wine: the exact amount of liqueuring varies, of course, each year, according to the quality of the grapes, but it usually has about $\frac{1}{4}$ per cent more than the driest champagnes. I often choose it when entertaining those who say that champagne is 'too acid', whilst finding it, myself, by no means unacceptably sweet.

The amount of liqueuring is expressed in terms of a percentage, but this is not, as is sometimes supposed, the amount of sugar as a percentage of the total amount of champagne. The percentage is worked out to a complicated technical formula but, very roughly, the figure is that of how many centilitres of the liqueur —half sugar, half old champagne—in the 78 centilitres that go to a bottle. The actual amount of *sugar* would be *half* the percentage figure.

Bollinger is a particularly dry wine, owing its fullness of flavour to the type and quality of the grapes and the firm's insistence on discarding the thinner pressings, and liqueuring is kept to the absolute minimum. As Mr Patrick Forbes observes,[8] 'In general it may be said that sweetening conceals the quality and masks the defects of a champagne; the really great ones are therefore seldom sweetened to any appreciable extent. . . .'

I have been told by the shipper of a very famous *marque* that no champagne is entirely without sugar: that such a wine would be unacceptably dry. He did not know his competitors' secrets, for Bollinger have done entirely without liqueuring on three occasions since the war—in 1947, in the R.D. 1959, and in one non-vintage blend. Its post-war average has been between $\frac{1}{2}$ and $\frac{3}{4}$ per cent, and in the 'big' year of 1964 it was only $\frac{1}{4}$ per cent.

This must make Bollinger unique. The most nearly comparable champagne to Bollinger in style is Krug, and M. Paul Krug told

[8] Patrick Forbes, op. cit.

Mr Edmund Penning-Rowsell of *The Financial Times* in 1965 that only once in this century had Krug added no *dosage* at all, and that was in the very hot year of 1904. In the past quarter-century, then, there have been three years when Bollinger added no *dosage*; not one such year for Krug. And if there have been no years since the war without *dosage* for Krug I cannot believe that there has been one for any other firm. Not every house is ready to give its figures, but it is a matter of pride to add only a very small *dosage*, and it would be a matter of even greater pride to be able to boast of having added none at all. It would mean that grapes only of the very highest quality had been used, picked at precisely the right point of ripeness, and the barest minimum of the later pressings accepted into the *cuvée*.

It is interesting to note that Krug added ½ per cent in 1959 and ¾ per cent in 1961. Leaving specific years aside, and looking at averages to compare with Bollinger's average over the years of between ½ and ¾ per cent, Mr Penning-Rowsell gave Pol Roger's average over recent years as 1¼ per cent, Moët et Chandon's 1½, Lanson 1¾ per cent. These are figures for the various houses' vintage wines: Lanson Black Label, the firm's non-vintage, is about 2, and I have no doubt that the *dosage* of the non-vintage wines of the other houses would also be higher than that of their vintage.

As I have said, many houses are more reluctant to give figures of *dosage* than those I have quoted, but I should say, on the strength of what I consider to be reasonably sound information gathered from a number of sources over many years, that over the *grandes marques* as a whole the average for the driest wines (labelled, as a rule, 'Brut' or 'Extra Dry') is about 1½ per cent. It will be seen, therefore, that Bollinger is liqueured about half as much as the general average.

Fully sweet champagnes (usually labelled 'Rich') run to about 4 per cent liqueuring. Not every house makes such a wine and some of those that are made are not exported to Britain. Bollinger, for instance, make a *Carte Blanche*, with a 4-per-cent *dosage*, but only for the South American market. This is much the same as those sweet champagnes that are sold on the British market—Lanson Rich and Veuve Clicquot Rich—and a little more than the Pol Roger Rich, which is more like 3½ per cent. All very modest compared with what I am told pre-revolutionary noblemen in St Petersburg used to demand—a champagne with a *dosage* of 12 per cent. One would have thought it would have stuck to the sides of the slippers of the Maryinsky ballerinas.

*   *   *

The second, and final, cork—the *bouchon d'expédition*—must be strong indeed: it will have to hold imprisoned, certainly for many months, possibly for some years, an atmospheric pressure of six atmospheres, or some 85 pounds to the square inch.

The classic champagne cork consists of *le manche*, or 'handle'— in its final compressed form, when the cork is in the bottleneck, this is the round top and also the neck of the cork—and the two or three *rondels* that form the base of the cork, inside the neck. The flat surface of the bottom *rondel*, in contact with the wine, is the *miroir*.

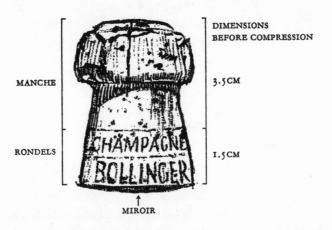

the second figure of the bottle, with labels: MANCHE, RONDELS, MIROIR, DIMENSIONS BEFORE COMPRESSION, 3.5CM, 1.5CM.

The laws of *appellation* require the word 'Champagne' to be stamped at some point on the *rondels*, near the *miroir*. And if it is a vintage wine, then the year is also required to be shown on the cork. Usually, the name of the house is stamped on the *miroir*.

Many—indeed most—of the great firms now use corks of which the *manche* is made of cork composition: cork that has been broken into granules that are then reconstituted as a solid.

This material is called in French *agglomeré*, the same noun that is used for compressed fuel, or briquettes.

Bollinger, though, use corks made all of natural cork, and it is interesting to note that, at the time of writing, these corks cost 42 centimes each, whereas the corks with a *manche* made of *agglomeré*, such as are to be popped from bottles of some of the most expensive and widely advertised premium brands of other houses, cost 27: the *agglomeré* can, of course, be made up of very poor quality cork. This in addition to the fact that Bollinger pay as much for their first cork as others do for their second—25 to 28 centimes compared with the 8 centimes that other houses pay for crown-corks. So for first and second corks together Bollinger pay 70 centimes on each bottle; many another house, though not quite all, pays exactly half that for both.

A cork such as Bollinger use is made of six or nine separate pieces, though they are so strongly and skilfully bonded together that the joins are virtually invisible. The *manche*, which, before being forced into the bottle, accounts for 3.5 cm of the total length of 5 cm, is made sometimes of two, sometimes of three pieces of solid cork, bonded vertically. Then two *rondels*, also each of either two or three pieces, also bonded vertically, but the joins of each *rondel* at right angles to the joins of the other, and none of them on the same axis as the joins of the *manche*. This method, of course, prevents seepage of wine through the cork.

All the cork is of good quality, but the bottom *rondel* is the finest of all, and shows no little holes or 'eyes' in its *miroir*; it is so cut with the grain that such very few 'eyes' as there are will be on the side and not on the base. But in the whole cylinder of a really good champagne cork there are very few 'eyes' indeed.

Finally, there is placed on the top of the cork the metal capsule that prevents the wire muzzle from cutting into it; the muzzle itself, to hold the cork in place; the label and the foil. So not only are the bubbles now firmly imprisoned in the bottle of Bollinger, but the bottle is dressed with appropriate dignity and style. After yet another three to six months' rest in the cellars, it sets off on its journey to the United Kingdom or the United States, Belgium or Brazil, and just as any distinguished human traveller is allowed, if possible, to rest after a journey, so is a bottle of good champagne; at whatever destination, the agents will give it a couple of months (in addition to the months it had after disgorgement) before sending it out to the wholesale firms, so that it arrives fit to do credit to a house that has gone to so much trouble over its quality.

7. Vineyard and Vine

OF the four directors of Bollinger, all related by blood or by marriage, one is both great-grandson of the original Jacques Bollinger and great-great-grandson of that Bollinger's father-in-law, Amiral Comte de Villermont.[1]

So when M. Yves Moret de Rocheprise took me round the Bollinger vineyards at Ay in the Vallée de la Marne, at Verzenay in the Montagne de Reims, and at Cuis in the Côte des Blancs, we were treading ground where his French great-great-grandfather (and earlier ancestors still) had been making wine a couple of centuries and more ago, the fame of which his Württemberger great-grandfather was the first to spread around Europe.

We have seen that many distinguished champagne houses, of which Krug is the outstanding example, own few vineyards of their own (Charles Heidsieck, indeed, own none at all), maintaining that their job is to make the best champagne they know how to make, and to leave growing grapes to those who know best how to do that quite different job.

[1] See chapter 4.

Others, such as Bollinger, maintain just as stoutly that this may have been all very well when more grapes were being grown than wine was being sold—when a great house could pick and choose from the supplies available, and be sure of a continuing supply, year after year, of the best grapes from the finest sites. And probably strike a buyer's bargain over them, at that.

Nowadays, no doubt, an old-established firm like Krug, that has dealt with the same vignerons for generations, still gets as good grapes as ever, and at the price fixed each year by the Comité Interprofessionel, representing all branches of the industry and the trade, and with government members to see fair play. All the same, it is reassuring in a changing world to know that some, at any rate, of one's supply of grapes is entirely under one's own control. And although, thanks to the Comité's fixed scale of agreed prices, there can be no profiteering in grapes by the independent vigneron, nevertheless, in a period of rising prices, the savings effected by growing one's own more than outweigh the very serious difficulties presented by shortage of labour in the vineyards. Indeed, Bollinger make no bones about saying that they wish they had vineyards enough of their own to supply all the grapes they need.[2]

This was the position they were in at the turn of the century, but the demand for all champagne has grown so much since then —the sales of Bollinger having increased at an even greater rate —that today the 270 acres of vineyards that belong to the house provide only between 40 and 45 per cent of the grapes required. Even so, this is one of the highest figures in Champagne: it is

[2] As this book was being prepared for the press, it was announced that an arrangement had been entered into by Bollinger, Krug, Roederer and Veuve Clicquot to co-ordinate their buying of grapes. This was widely misunderstood, especially in France. M. Christian Bizot assured me that each firm would continue to buy the grapes it had always bought, from the areas in which it had always bought them: all that the arrangement meant was that in years when there is a shortage, and only then, the four firms would buy jointly in the areas, and only in the areas, where all four had traditionally bought in the past. There is no financial or commercial link between the firms, and none is envisaged: the main reason, as M. Bizot puts it, being 'more psychological, giving us more weight in the crazy race that sometimes happens to get good grapes in poor years'.

probable that only three other houses, Roederer, Taittinger and the small firm of Henriot, out of the 144 houses each with a brand name (or a number of brand names) of its own have a higher percentage of their own grapes in their blends.[3] Many, as we have seen, have none.

Bollinger are proud to own as many vineyards as they do—each marked as is the custom in Champagne with the name of the house on the little boundary stone so like a gravestone that one American visitor was going around constantly baring his head until he began to wonder at so many people of the same name being interred in so scattered a fashion over the countryside.

Each vineyard, however small, has its name in the books. It is easy to guess how some derive: Côte aux Enfants, Voie aux Vaches, Champ du Clerc; but some are bizarre, like Faubourg d'Enfer; some fanciful, such as Les Gouttes d'Or and Les Aumonières. And one wonders what long-ago countryman gave Froid-Cul and Pisse-Renard their names, and why.

To be a vineyard-owner as well as a champagne-maker certainly gives an extra dimension to Madame Bollinger's life, for she cycles daily through the vineyards, coming early into the tasting-room with news of a promising flowering or warnings of this or that of the many sicknesses that can befall the vine. It is impossible to guess how she would fill her day without vines to inspect as well as wines to taste.

In a good year, Bollinger—like any other successful champagne house—would be glad to buy more grapes than in other years, and if necessary to outbid other firms to get them, and to get the best.

But the whole structure of the champagne industry is too tightly knit for this to be possible, and Bollinger are lucky in being so famous a firm that most of the grapes they have to buy are bought from growers with whom they have been dealing since the beginning of the century—not only serious growers, but almost family friends.

Each house is permitted its share of the year's total output of

[3] I exclude co-operatives, such as Mailly, in which of course the grapes all come from members' own vineyards, but none of which, good though its wine may be, ranks as a *grande marque.*

grapes, based on previous purchases, and at the fixed prices already referred to, decided upon by the Comité, in agreement with makers and growers.

Not that this means that all grapes in Champagne are sold at the same price—far from it. The whole *vignoble* of the Marne is graded so as to show the value of each of 180 communes' grapes (each parish's, as it were) as a percentage of the very top class. This *échelle*, or grading, was first made officially by the Comité in 1945, but it is based on agreed published scales going back at least as far as 1911, after the Champagne riots, and has been subject to minor revisions since.

Thus, each year at vintage time, only one price need be agreed —that of the highest, or 100 per cent category. The percentage of that price, whatever it is, that the grapes of any particular vine-yard can command are already fixed: this one at 90 per cent, another at 75 per cent. The small outlying regions of the Aisne and the Aube, the inclusion and then the exclusion of which caused so much trouble in 1911, are graded at the bottom, but these are relatively unimportant: the three areas of the Marne— Montagne, Vallée and Côte des Blancs—provide more than 80 per cent of all the grapes used for champagne, and all the grapes used by the best houses.

Obviously, the scale cannot be perfect. Within each commune there will be some vineyards that are superior to others—perhaps immediately contiguous—because of slight advantages of slope, exposure or drainage. But it would be virtually impossible— certainly unwieldy—further to subdivide a list that already in-cludes no fewer than 180 Marne place-names, five from the Aisne and a category for the Aube. And the scale is remarkably fair, as can be realized from the fact that it is very rare indeed for a vigneron to apply for a new assessment.

As it is, the *échelle* for 1969, given as Appendix IV, shows that a few communes carry different gradings for black and for white grapes—not many, as very few areas grow both. The Côte is virtually all white grapes, the Montagne and the Vallée virtually all black: that is what the soil of each district dictates. And there is a premium within each category for the black Pinot Noir and the white Chardonnay over the other permitted strains, the

Meunier, the Arbanne and the Petit Meslier. Although granted no premium, the Meunier is widely used (though not by Bollinger), but the Arbanne and the Petit Meslier survive only in such less-favoured regions as the Aube. They are going out of production and, although not forbidden, are not being replanted: they account for less than 1 per cent of the region's vines.

Altogether, with the various premiums and surcharges, the 4.14 fr. a kilogram laid down as the basic price in 1969 for the 100 per cent growths became in practice 4.85 fr.—a sizeable price when one remembers that it takes 1.66 kilograms, or more than eight francs' worth, to make a bottle of champagne. One sympathized with M. de Rocheprise on the day the 1969 vintage opened when, walking with me through the vineyards, he clapped his hands to frighten away a great, greedy flock of starlings: 'They're too damned expensive, at four francs eighty-five a kilo!'

Expensive indeed for Bollinger, whose own vineyards are rated as follows:

				Approximate area
Ay	100 per cent			21·3 hectares
Bisseuil	93 ,, ,,			5·3 ,,
Bouzy	100 ,, ,,			*
Cuis	95 ,, ,,	(white grapes)		20 ,,
Grauves	93 ,, ,,	(white grapes)		11·5 ,,
Louvois	100 ,, ,,			*
Tauxières	99 ,, ,,			*
Verzenay	100 ,, ,,			17 ,,

* The Bouzy, Louvois and Tauxières vineyards together: 31·2—the average rate of which is much higher than would be obtained by adding the first column of figures and dividing by eight, which gives 97·5 per cent: as will be seen from the second column the acreage of Bollinger's 93 per cent vineyards is very much smaller than that of the 99 and 100 per cent.

It is easy to see why Bollinger, dedicated to quality as they are, think it so important to be vineyard-owners, as well as champagne-makers. These vineyards provide the same foundation each year on which to build a wine of the Bollinger 'style'—not only is quality thus assured, but also a continuity of character, especially as such a high proportion is in the classic Ay *vignoble*.

Bollinger also buy from eleven other communes, seven of which rate either 99 or 100 per cent, and only one of which, Venteuil, at 85, falls below 93 per cent.

The average percentage of top-scale price paid by Bollinger each year is 97, probably as high as, or higher than, that paid by any other house in Champagne. There must be houses that buy only in the Aube, the Aisne, and the cheaper communes of the Marne, to show an average of between 75 and 80 per cent, and there can be no house with an average of 100 per cent. For one thing, there are not enough grapes in the top category for one house to deal with them exclusively; for another, all good champagne needs some, at any rate, of the less fine, less delicate grapes, to give balance to the finished wine. It cannot be stated too often that champagne is a *blended* wine—blended not only of black and white grapes, but of grapes from different parts of the region and of different character, so that the wine will be rounded, full of champagne 'character', complete, and long-lived. Bollinger count themselves lucky to have had for the past seventy years a source of supply in Venteuil of Pinot Meunier grapes that have a greater finesse than most growths of this variety, and which fit well into the Bollinger style, adding a touch of robustness without the *gout de terroir*—raciness of the soil—detectable in most wines of this strain from communes in the 85 per cent category.

This is perhaps the place to point out the various ways in which producers can save money in making their wine and why some champagnes are dearer than others. As it takes some 1.66 kilograms of grapes at 4.85 fr. to make a bottle of wine, the difference in cost per bottle between a producer who pays, say, an average of 95 per cent for his grapes and one who pays 75 is 1.60 fr., say twelve pence. And the difference in cost to the consumer is, of course, greater by the percentage of profit added to this by shipper, importer, wholesaler and retailer.

We have already seen that some firms, such as Bollinger, use only the first and sometimes, but not always, the second pressings of juice—the *vin de cuvée* or *tête de cuvée* and sometimes the *première taille*—whereas other firms buy from them the *deuxième taille* or third pressing, which is entitled by law to be called champagne, but which is a thinner wine altogether.

We saw, too, in the same chapter, that by using a crown-cork for the *bouchon de tirage* and one largely made of compressed granulated cork for the *bouchon d'expédition*, a saving of some thirty-five centimes a bottle can be effected on this small item alone—about 2½p a bottle, say, to the producer, which becomes more like 5p by the time it has reached the consumer.

And there are many other economies to be made by using metal instead of wood, by installing modern machinery, and by turning out one's champagne as soon as the law allows rather than give it the maturing time you feel yourself to be necessary. Now this does not necessarily mean that the cheapest of the *grandes marques* have been made of inferior grapes from communes the grapes of which are classed at from 75 per cent, and third pressings bought from neighbouring houses more dedicated to quality. There are very many more champagnes than the *grandes marques*. Some of the very biggest of the *grandes marques* firms have undoubtedly brought down costs by rationalization, by improved methods of distribution, by severe pruning of overheads, and by capital investment in modern plant made possible by the volume of their sales.

What it does mean, though, is that the very best champagnes (and I am by no means referring only to Bollinger)—those that will not economize by lowering their standards, and will not adopt modern methods unless they are satisfied that quality will not suffer—must necessarily be among the most expensive.

Apart from the *grandes marques*, there are the B.O.B.—buyers' own brand—champagnes sold under their own labels by old-established wine-merchants in this country, as well as by department stores, grocers and supermarkets. Then there are the brands sold only by the French grocers and self-service stores, which are never seen in Britain. These, too, vary enormously. Some may be made by small *manipulants* from their own vineyards, some perhaps made very well, some very badly.

There are big firms that specialize in B.O.B. champagnes, certainly not made from the most expensive grapes, certainly not made exclusively from first pressings, and certainly not kept longer than is necessary in the cellar, but some, again, well-made. At best, they are lighter than the best champagnes, not made to be kept for long; at worst, they are acid and astringent.

There are two ways of regarding the difference between the best (which generally speaking, but not absolutely necessarily, means the most expensive) champagne and the cheaper B.O.B. and grocers' wines, amongst which, of course, the better are, again as a rule, the more expensive.

One can spurn the cheaper as poor stuff, or one can hold that the strict laws of *appellation* ensure that there is no such thing as a *bad* champagne—merely·that some are very much better than others. I have certainly enjoyed some good B.O.B. champagnes myself from reputable firms (the wine club of which I am chairman sells one), though I would not class them as the finest wines I have ever drunk; I have not enjoyed so much some of the bottles of cheap champagne I have bought in French supermarkets, though I suppose they would make good enough Black Velvet, or Buck's Fizz.[4]

On the whole, in champagnes as in so much else, one gets what one pays for: what I have tried to indicate here is why. . . .

* * *

It was late one February that I first visited the Bollinger vineyards. It was cold, with sparse, dry snowflakes floating, rather than falling, in the still air. Columns of smoke rose quite straight from between the lines of stakes where men in faded blue denim suits, cloth caps and rubber boots were burning the prunings from the vines.

Three methods of pruning are permitted to vines entitled to the champagne *appellation*—methods designed to ensure quality by restricting production. In the Bollinger vineyards only two of these three are used—the *taille de Royat* for the Pinot Noir (black grapes) and the *taille de Chablis* for the white Chardonnay—because the third system, the Guyot, is not permitted to the highest category vineyards.

Appellation laws are always strict, and in no respect more so than in the matter of pruning: so many inches from the ground; only so many shoots, so many inches apart; only so many buds

---

[4] See chapter 9.

to the shoot. In a normal year, it is possible to forecast almost to an ounce what weight of grapes and volume of juice a hectare of vineyard will yield: pruning has decided quite precisely the number of bunches.

But there are two tiny exceptions to what I have just written, for Bollinger own two small pre-phylloxera vineyards.

As explained in chapter 5, the vineyards of Champagne were devastated, roughly over the twenty years from 1890 to 1910, by *phylloxera vastatrix*, the plant louse that kills the vine at the root.

The answer to this plague, in Champagne as in the rest of the wine-growing world, from the Rhine to the Murrumbidgee, was to graft the classic vines of Europe on to the phylloxera-resistant stock of the native American vine. All the finest vines of the world now grow on American roots. In Champagne the war interrupted the process, which was not completed until the middle 1920s.

Here and there, though, in the world's various wine-growing areas, are vineyards that freakishly escaped the plague, ranging in size from the whole of the wine-growing area of Chile, isolated between the Andes and the Pacific, by way of some fairly substantial port-growing slopes in the Douro, to the two of which I now write—two vineyards owned by Bollinger, one of one-third of a hectare, the other of one-sixth, half a hectare in all, or about one and a quarter acres.

These vineyards, in the Montagne de Reims, are planted with Pinot Noir, and the vines are permitted to be grown and pruned as they always were, before the phylloxera came, and the strict application of the laws of *appellation*, with the restrictions that necessarily go with them. They are planted *en foule*, which is to say higgledy-piggledy, growing vertically up stakes, and not trained horizontally along wires, and they create new vines by 'layering'. This is the system by which each vine is pruned so that there remains only one branch, which is trained underground to protrude above the soil some feet away from its parent vine. The buried portion puts down roots, so that a new vine is created, and the operation is repeated so that the vineyard is constantly renewing itself and getting progressively more untidy.

Vines grown and trained in this way remain vigorous, producing good grapes and good wine, to the age of seventy and more, compared with the thirty or so that is the limit for the grafted vines of today, trained and pruned as the law requires. Indeed, when Charles Walter Berry, of Berry Bros., visited Champagne in 1934, Jacques Bollinger took him to see another pre-phylloxera vineyard that Bollinger then owned at Bouzy, and told him that some of the vines then were 100 to 120 years old. This is why, as will be seen in chapter 8, it was possible for Bollinger to make good champagne in 1969 from these *vieilles vignes françaises*, which must certainly date from before the First World War.

This wine is a unique exception, though, and Bollinger's two little pre-phylloxera vineyards are freaks of nature.

It would be out of the question now for vines to be planted or layered in this way, because it would mean that they would be particularly vulnerable to the phylloxera: as we have seen, new vines are produced only by grafting on to resistant American stock. (This protects not only the grower concerned, but all his neighbours and, indeed, all his fellow-countrymen and even fellow-Europeans: the phylloxera spreads.)

Nor would it any longer be economically possible. By the *en foule* system, vines stray and straggle all over the place, making it impossible to use machinery in the vineyards, in the way that it is used now through the trim, neat rows of carefully trained vines.

Nowadays, various kinds of spider-like *tracteurs enjambeurs* straddle the vines—in the winter, to turn the soil and bank it up over the stems of the vines; in the summer for the half-dozen to a dozen or more sprayings to which the vines must be subjected if they are to be protected against mildew, oïdium, and the various ticks and larvae that attack leaves and fruit. It is the copper-sulphate sprayings, against the mildew, that give the vine-leaves the hard, metallic, blue-green tinge so familiar to those who drive through the vineyards of France in high summer.

In the small vineyards, owned by peasant proprietors, men still do the spraying by hand, from tanks strapped to their backs, though many small men will combine to hire a tractor between them.

The bigger firms, though, combine now to introduce yet

another machine. In the wet June of 1969, in the Montagne de Reims, I saw a helicopter spraying Bollinger's vineyards against the mildew, because the rains had made the heavy ground too muddy for the tractors, but the vines that much more liable to the disease. The pilot, with a Battle of Britain moustache, touched down every few minutes to refill his tanks of spray, and then was off again, banking and turning, banking and turning— frighteningly low, it seemed, especially after one had been told of the helicopter that had caught its undercarriage in the wires supporting the vines, and crashed. On that occasion, although a vast amount of expensive damage was done to the vines, the pilot had not been killed—but he could well have been.

There is nothing, though, that machines can do for the vigneron at the climax of his year—the vintage.

It is autumn now. The leaves are so thick on the vines that unless one looks right along the rows they seem to cover the slopes in a solid mass—dark green, because they are only just beginning to turn colour, freckling the landscape as yet only here and there with bronze and yellow and red.

The rows are gaily untidy with fluttering coloured rags, ripped from fertilizer bags, and with glittering strips of tinsel, to scare away the birds, which—a rare thing in France—it is forbidden to shoot, because they pick the parasites off the sheep and cows of the region's dairy-farmers.

Speckling the vineyards now are the cloth caps and the berets of the men, their faded blue denims, and the younger lads' coloured shirts, the head-scarves of the girls and the white *bagnolets*—cotton or linen poke-bonnets—that a few of the older women still affect. For to pick grapes the human hand is necessary: picking machines may be all very well for hops, but even if they could be adapted to picking grapes how could they fail to damage the bloom on their skins? And the bloom is the natural yeasts that bring about fermentation.

What is more, in top-category vineyards such as Bollinger's, and those that Bollinger buy from, each bunch of grapes is examined so that bruised, imperfect and unripe grapes can be rejected: this system of *épluchage* is beyond the most cunning machine yet invented.

In Bollinger's own 270 acres of vineyards, the permanent staff of eighty is augmented for the couple of weeks or so of the vintage by 300 tough townsfolk from the grim mining area of Lille-Roubaix, some of them immigrant Polish colliers whose Polish-cum-northern-French accent baffles the *champenois*.

They are brought by motor-coach, the same families every year, just as the same London families used to come year after year to pick the Kentish hops, before the machines took over and the extra money had become less important to the cockney anyway. No locals come, from Reims or Epernay.

But the hop-pickers never lived so well as these *vendangeurs* from the pits of northern France. Strategically placed among their vineyards, Bollinger have six houses, each a dormitory-refectory for some fifty of them, used only during the vintage. Some of the big firms put up great marquees at vintage time, others have solid buildings like Bollinger's, but let them off to youth clubs at other times of the year. Bollinger's buildings lie unprofitably empty for fifty weeks in the year, which is unbusinesslike of the firm—and it is not one of those extravagances that adds to the quality of their wine as well as to its price.

The one I visited during the 1969 vintage was spartanly austere, spotlessly clean, everything scrubbed to within an inch of its life. In the kitchen that morning, women were preparing potatoes, cabbage and leeks, and chopping parsley, for the evening meal, where in England the packets of peas would not yet have left the deep-freeze.

The workers had had coffee at seven that morning—picking always begins early, when the grapes are cool, to cut down the amount of grapes liable to ferment in the heat of the day on the way to the press-house. At a quarter to nine, they had had bread and pâté of pig's liver, with red wine or lemonade, taken out to them in the vineyards, and I can vouch for the lunch they had on that particular day, for I shared it with one group in the Montagne de Reims, sitting with the *vendangeurs* at a trestle-table between the vines. I was served a mountainous helping of savoury ragout of pork, rich with herbs and haricot beans, hot in an insulated canister from the car that had brought it from the kitchen, accompanied by excellent crusty bread, baked that morning, followed by triangles of cheese in silver-paper (the only item in the meal to remind me of an English harvest home) and a big juicy pear, and we washed it all down with red wine— *vin ordinaire* of the lowest alcoholic strength, 8.5 degrees, to be permitted to be called wine.

There would be bread, cheese, coffee and red wine at half-past three, and that evening, at seven, my companions were to dine on soup, tongue, the vegetables I had seen being prepared, cheese and coffee and cake, and more red wine—not so elegantly as I would dine at the 'Berceaux' in Epernay, where I was staying, with its excellent starred restaurant, but at least as heartily. Always meat three times a day, at breakfast, lunch and supper, besides coffee at getting-up time and at mid-afternoon. A typical Bollinger menu shows, as its main dishes only, brawn for breakfast, hot roast beef for lunch and tripe for supper.

The last dinner of the vintage is always the traditional *cochelet*, named after the sucking-pig that used to be, but is no longer, its main course. The pig has gone, to be replaced by great helpings of pâté and of chicken, but the champagne remains—it is always a great feast, the *cochelet*; there is always champagne with it; and next morning every *vendangeur* takes two free bottles of champagne back with him to cheer him up in his drab colliery town.

Apart from the hearty food and the barrack-like but exquisitely clean accommodation, the actual pickers are paid 25 francs for an eight-and-a-half hour day, the porters who carry what they pick to the lorries 36—taking back the equivalent of somewhere between £25 and £50 for their fortnight's work, or what is left of it after adding to their two free bottles of champagne, and buying presents for their families at home. For these folk are not badly off these days: they come to the vintage not so much for the money as for the food, the fresh air and the companionship—and they come already hung with cameras and transistor sets.

That year, 1969, '*nous décuidons*', said M. Moret de Rocheprise —'we're making less'. The crop was some 10 to 20 per cent less than had been expected, and what had been expected was less than what was needed. The flowering had been poor, and although the grapes provided both juice and sugar of good quality, they were small.

Quantity is always a problem in Champagne, as well as quality. Bollinger, for instance, hold at present about five and a half million bottles of champagne. Each year they sell about a million. Each year wine must be made—vintage wine in a good year, non-vintage in a poor year, when heavier demands will be made on the wines held in reserve. Unless Bollinger can bottle as much each year as they sell, or average this over fairly short periods of years, the stocks will decline: it is easy to see that it would take only a short unbroken period, not even of really bad, but of merely poorish years so to reduce stocks that they might have to ration their customers. It has happened in the past, and although it might be argued that it enhances the prestige of a product for it to be hard to get—Wilkinson razor-blades spring to mind—no champagne-maker likes to see old customers drinking the wine of rival firms because they cannot get his own. There are many good champagnes about: some might become, as it were, habit-forming.

8. Vintage, Non-Vintage and the Rest

'THE best champagne is a balanced wine,' I wrote in a previous chapter, 'because it is a blended wine.'

Madame Bollinger and her colleagues and cellar-staff would go further than this: indeed, I have heard Madame Bollinger say, not that the *best* champagne is a blended wine, but simply, comprehensively and flatly that, 'champagne is a blended wine' and, moreover, add pointedly that it is a white one.

The point being that although a number of distinguished houses make a *blanc de blancs* champagne, and a few make a *rosé*, there are those *champenois* purists—and Madame Bollinger is very much, and very articulately, a *champenoise* purist—who stick firmly to the principle: champagne is a sparkling white wine made from a blend of the juice of black and of white grapes and, come to that, of more black than white, from more than one vineyard and more than one district in the region—black from more than one, and white from more than one.

The argument in favour of a *blanc de blancs* champagne put forward by those who disagree with her is well-known, and goes something like this: In the typical blend for the classic champagne of must from black and from white grapes, it is the black grapes that give body and fruit, the white grapes delicacy and finesse. Therefore, a wine made from the must of white grapes only will necessarily be *all* delicacy and finesse.

It should be made clear that the term *blanc de blancs* is not an *appellation controlée*, has no legal validity, and is subject to no checks on its authenticity, so that there are those cynics in the trade who say that all that is needed to make it is to give the appropriate instructions to the printer of one's labels.

But I have drunk various brands of *blanc de blancs* champagne that I am sure were precisely what their producers said they were; I have accepted the explanation that they were rather more expensive than the usual blend of *blanc et noir* because their greater delicacy needed considerable skill in the making, as well as because white grapes are needed for the blends, and are expensive to use on their own; and I have found some of them truly delicious.

Nor am I alone in this. So good a judge of wine in general and of champagne in particular as André Simon has written of *blanc de blancs*, 'dry and elegant, it is an ideal wine to serve before a meal, or as the first wine of the day in the forenoon after a late night'.[1]

Two other members of the same generation, now deceased, were similarly enthusiastic: Warner Allen (who called it 'Blanc de Blanc') wrote[2] that there was never 'a finer example' of 'lightness, delicacy and finesse', and said that it was the favourite wine of C. W. Berry, the distinguished wine-merchant of the first decades of the century, who wrote enthusiastically about it in his *In Search of Wine*, published in 1935.

To which the reply of those of the Bollinger school of thought is something like: 'it may be all you say it is; it may well be delicious; but it is not precisely what *we* call champagne'. And, oddly enough, it is a much younger writer than André Simon—

---

[1] André Simon, *The History of Champagne*, 1962.
[2] Warner Allen, *White Wines and Cognac*, 1952.

Mr Hugh Johnson—who has vigorously expressed the more austere, old-fashioned, point of view:

> Classical champagne is a blend of these two regions [i.e. the white-grape and the black-grape country]. Each has something to offer the other. Recently, however, champagne made of the juice of white grapes alone, called *blanc de blancs*, has come on to the market, under the guise of being lighter than the traditional kind. I have not met anyone who has found the old kind of champagne too heavy, but the power of suggestion is great, and since 'lighter' Scotch has been such a success, and lighter rum and drier gin and vodka—with no taste at all —have all proved extremely popular, it seems a reasonable assumption that the public would swallow the same thing with champagne.
>
> It is usually sold at a higher price than classical champagne, though in what way it can be worth more it is hard to say; white grapes are no more expensive than black ones. It is, in fact, a fashion, which will eventually stand or fall on its merits. But it is a pity that anyone should be misled into thinking that no champagne is good enough unless it is *blanc de blancs*.[3]

Mr Johnson is not quite right in saying that white grapes are no more expensive than black. There is a relative shortage, over the whole region, of white grapes, and thus a higher demand than for, at any rate, the lower-category black. There are no Côte des Blancs vineyards so low in the Comité's price-scale as the cheapest black-grape vineyards, so the average price is higher, and in any case it is only the grapes from the best white-grape vineyards that can be used for a good *blanc de blancs*. What is more, it cannot be made at all in poor years, as a non-vintage blend can be, and is. In such years, unblended with wines from black grapes that would smooth over their sharp acidity, they are harsh and unappealing.

That apart, though, his is much the same point of view as I

[3] Hugh Johnson, *Wine*, London, 1966. The quotations from Warner Allen, C. W. Berry and André Simon make it clear that the development is not so recent as Mr Johnson supposed. But it is true that especially vigorous marketing of *blanc de blancs* is a fairly recent development.

have heard expressed in the Bollinger tasting-room, though there, perhaps, it is expressed a little more moderately, for the Bollinger directors do not like to appear to be criticizing their competitors: they would rather say, in effect, '*this* is the way we think it right to do things here', than say, '*that's* the way they do it at so-and-so's, and it's wrong'.

But I think they might well go so far as to say with Mr Patrick Forbes, himself managing director of Moët et Chandon's London house, who, after a warning word about authenticity, points out that 'many Champenois consider true champagne *blanc de blancs* too light a wine, lacking "follow through"; its taste, they say, vanishes with undue haste, without leaving champagne's characteristic imprint on the palate and the throat'.[4]

Maurice Renoir, the seventy-five-year-old vigneron whom I have already quoted says, speaking out of more than sixty years' experience of growing, making, and drinking champagne, that *blanc de blancs* lacks body, adding that 'to make a good champagne, you must make a good *mélange*'—making it clear that the *mélange* must be of black and white.

So, although it may be that some or all of the Bollinger directors have been given an occasional crisply refreshing and appetizing glass of *blanc de blancs* before dinner at a rival family's evening party, and probably enjoyed it, nevertheless they do not regard it as part of their job to produce such a wine of their own: what the house of Bollinger sets out to do is to produce the traditional type of champagne by the traditional methods—and this excludes the relatively new-fangled *blanc de blancs*. So, too, with *rosé*, which I prefer to call, simply, pink champagne.

Pink champagne is far from being new-fangled, and has a much longer history than *blanc de blancs*—carries with it, indeed, the trailing glories of late-Victorian and Edwardian frivolity and fun, a tradition already getting on for a century old, so that it is old-fashioned rather than new-fangled, and a fashion, in fact, dying out rather than coming in. Nevertheless, the Bollinger face so far has always been set against it. Champagne, says Madame firmly, is a white wine.

[4] Patrick Forbes, *Champagne*, 1967.

There are three ways of making pink champagne, two of them legitimate.

It can be made by leaving the juice of the black grapes for longer on the skins than usual—though not so long, of course, as for a fully red wine. This is the classic method by which the best still *rosés* are made, but very few, if any, champagne houses now favour it, as it is difficult to control the colour thus obtained or to be sure of its eventual development in a sparkling wine.

It can be made by adding to the white wine a proportion of the still red wine of the region—probably from Bouzy—and this, I think, is now the universal practice.

Made even in this latter way, pink champagne is expensive, because the stability of the colour is still uncertain, though less so than when it is obtained by leaving the juice on the skins. It can still fade in the bottle, or turn a pale tawny, or 'onion-skin' colour. The process is risky, and risks have to be paid for.

The third, illegitimate, method is to add cochineal, or some other colouring agent. No reputable Champagne firm would do this, even if it were permitted: it *may* be done with other sparkling wines in other countries, or even in other regions of France.

Now it must not be supposed that, because pink champagne looks pretty and carries overtones of frivolity, it is sweet. It could, of course, be made sweet, as any champagne can be, but by its nature it is fuller-flavoured, harder and drier than the classic golden champagne: it may very well be longer-lived in bottle. Even if it were made sweet, this fullness of flavour would still be there, behind the sweetness, and so could well be the greater staying-power. For obviously, as it is the juice of the black grape that gives body to the classic wine, there will be more body still if, in addition to the juice, there is an extract from the skins. Also from the skins comes the tannin that gives dryness and staying power to a red wine—astringency, even, until it mellows with age in bottle.

So the *champenois* purist's argument against pink champagne is that although it may be regarded by some as femininely pretty to the eye, it is, in fact, hard and masculine to the taste. Maurice Renoir told me that he always detected 'a taste of gooseberry' in even the best pink champagne, by which, I think, he meant not sourness but an asperity not found in the traditional golden wine —an element of tannin from the skins of the black grapes.

The way that Mr Patrick Forbes puts the feelings towards pink champagne of the maker of the traditional wine of the region— and this in spite of the fact that his own firm, Moët et Chandon, makes a vintage pink champagne, and a good one—is that, 'he considers it alien to the mainstream of his destiny'.[5]

That is certainly the feeling at Bollinger, where they have never made a pink champagne. They could perhaps be persuaded by an influential agent, as Moët et Chandon were persuaded, that there existed a demand for a pink Bollinger, which it would be improper or imprudent to ignore. In which case, I am sure, they would make as good a *rosé* as anyone in Champagne. I am equally sure that Madame's heart would not be in it.

*   *   *

Bollinger make four wines. They are all white, they are all blends of the juice of black grapes and of white, and although the proportion may vary from one year to another according to the style and quality of the vintage, it will not vary *within* the year, for each wine is made to the house style—every wine, basically, is of the same quality. Every wine is Bollinger.

Take, for instance, Bollinger Carte Blanche, a wine unknown in Europe, for it is not to the European taste—a sweet champagne specially liqueured for the South American market, and sold only in South America. But it is in no way an inferior product: it is made in precisely the same way as Bollinger is for the European market, of the same quality grapes, and in the same proportions. The only difference between it and other Bollinger champagnes is that at the liqueuring stage (see chapter 6) the *dosage* of sugar-and-wine syrup is 4 per cent as against the Bollinger average for its other wines of between $\frac{1}{2}$ and $\frac{3}{4}$ per cent —sometimes none at all. But the wine is still of the true Bollinger breed.

As already explained, more than half the Bollinger champagne produced, averaged over the years, is the non-vintage

[5] Patrick Forbes, op. cit.

wine. In fact, this is seldom referred to as such, and never thus labelled.

In June 1911, a circular letter was sent to all their customers by Mentzendorff & Co., Bollinger's London agents:

> Dear Sirs,
>
> Mr Bollinger having decided, from this date, to have the words 'Special Cuvée' printed on his label of Non-Vintage Wine, we shall be glad if you will, when revising your list, quote this Wine as 'Bollinger, Special Cuvée, Very Dry'.
>
> Thanking you in anticipation, etc.

Mr Bollinger is credited with the decision, but one is told, not only at the Mentzendorff office in London but at the Bollinger house in Ay, that it was the bright idea of Arthur William ('Toby') Folks, then a partner in Mentzendorff, to drop the term 'non-vintage', and designate the house's non-vintage wine as 'special cuvée'. This is how it has been styled ever since, and customers who ask for Bollinger 'N.V.', as they would order the non-vintage wine of any other house, are always answered with a tactful reference to 'Bollinger S.C.'.

No one, of course, makes any secret of the fact that it *is* non-vintage: there is no intent to deceive. But it was felt then, and is still felt, that to call it 'special cuvée' gives a defensible indication of the care that goes into its making. It is certainly true that sales in the United Kingdom went up with the change of style, and have stayed up: a rose by another name is not necessarily sweeter, but may sell better. Many houses now give their non-vintage wine a brand name: Pol Roger 'White Foil', Lanson 'Black Label', Krug 'Private Cuvée Brut Réserve', and the like.

In any case, there is a sense in which non-vintage champagne, of any of the great houses, is really the true, classic wine in that, being essentially a blend, it reflects the ideas, ideals and character of the people who make it. For their choice of how much black and how much white, from which vineyards of what region, how much of one year's reserves and how much of another, is a more deliberate expression of the personality of their house than is possible in their vintage champagne, where some of the character is imposed by influences over which they have no control.

Vintage champagne is also, of course, a blended wine in that it is made of black and white grapes from different vineyards: but it is made of the grapes of one year's vintage only. It must be a 'good' year—which can, but does not necessarily, mean a plentiful year, but must mean a year that produced grapes of fine quality: all fully ripe at vintage time, with plenty of sugar and flavour in the fruit. This means a richer, but not, of course, a sweeter wine, for the sugar is converted by fermentation into alcohol—heavier in style, fuller in flavour. It will not only reflect the style of the house that made it, but also the character of the year: a very full, rich 1959, for instance, or a much lighter and more delicate 1952 or 1962.

So whereas the Bollinger special cuvée is unique, solely and specifically a Bollinger creation, and unlike any other champagne; the 1959, say, or 1962 vintage Bollinger will share characteristics of those particular years, to however slight a degree, with the 1959 or the 1962 of other great houses.

A firm such as Bollinger is immensely proud of its vintage wine—almost 40 per cent of the total output of Bollinger, indeed, is vintage champagne, compared with the average over the whole trade of a mere 15 per cent—and yet there is a sense in which I feel that the directors are prouder, if that were possible, of their special cuvée. It requires even greater skill and subtlety in the blending and making (as a rule, that is: there are occasional 'difficult' vintage years), and it reflects even more precisely the character and personality of its makers. Bollinger 1959 is not only 'Bollinger' but also '1959' in character: Bollinger special cuvée is all Bollinger.

Why then do the great firms trouble to make a vintage champagne at all, and why is it dearer than non-vintage?

Although it is hard to get any champagne-maker to say as much or, at any rate, to say it for quotation, I believe that many of the finest houses would be glad to devote all their skill and all their resources to producing the best non-vintage wines they are capable of producing; to have the fine wine of vintage years in reserve to blend with, and to better, the non-vintage; and to be judged by them.

Each *grande marque* house produces a vintage wine in a vintage year because its rivals do, and because it is a means of getting talked and written about. It is dearer than non-vintage because it takes up so much of the highest quality wines that would otherwise make it easier to blend the non-vintage.

When the Bollinger 1962 or, say, the Pol Roger 1964, is launched, there are tastings for the trade and for the press, in Britain, in the United States, and elsewhere, probably with Madame Bollinger or Madame Pol Roger herself present. The wine's appearance on the market is announced in the trade journals, commented on in the Sunday newspapers and the glossy magazines: the name of Bollinger or of Pol Roger appears in print whereas, if there were never a vintage, it might (or so it is feared) have to be heavily and expensively advertised, or be forgotten.

This would not be so, of course, if all the champagne houses agreed, at the same time, to abandon the making of vintage wines, and all go in solely for non-vintage. But who can imagine all the champagne houses agreeing on any one thing, all at the same time?

Meanwhile, in a vintage year such as 1962 or 1964, Bollinger will make only a vintage wine, whereas most—perhaps all—other houses will always make some non-vintage every year.

The fact that in a good year all the firm's efforts go to making a vintage wine does not mean that all the year's wine also goes into it: as explained in chapter 6, reserves of the best wines of good years are put away in magnums so that they can be drawn upon in poor years to blend into good special cuvée, or non-vintage, wine.

Besides declaring with a flourish the appearance of each vintage wine, a custom common to all the major champagne houses, some firms have each taken a further step towards attracting publicity and—they hope—acquiring prestige: the production and promotion of what Mr Patrick Forbes calls 'super-de-luxe' brands. These are champagnes that are said to be superior to the vintage wines of each house, as the vintage is superior to the non-vintage, and appropriately more expensive still.

Some, like the Dom Pérignon of Mr Forbes's own distinguished firm, are blended differently from other wines of the same house: Dom Pérignon is said to reverse the usual proportions of black grapes and white, and be (it may vary a little, according to the year) about 75 per cent white, 25 black—almost a *blanc de blancs.*

Others, like the Taittinger 'Comtes de Champagne', are, in fact, *blanc de blancs*; others are said to be *tête de cuvée*—made only from the first pressing of the grapes (see chapter 6) whereas even the usual *grande marque* champagne takes along with the juice of the first pressing the first two casks of the second pressing to add character and body to the first.

There is usually a bigger jump in price from vintage to premium quality, or 'super-de-luxe' than from non-vintage: at the time of writing, the non-vintage Moët et Chandon is £1.90; the vintage £2.40; and the Dom Pérignon £3.64. It is worth remembering that the duty, both in France and abroad, is exactly the same on all sparkling wine, whether non-vintage, vintage, or de luxe: thus, the actual price differential is proportionately greater than it appears.

Some of these *de luxe* wines are most beautifully packaged and presented: Dom Pérignon, in a replica of an eighteenth-century champagne bottle with its pastiche of an eighteenth-century label, must be the most handsome bottle of wine in the world, and the Roederer Cristal Brut, in the clear-glass bottle that Tsars used to insist upon, is historically interesting as well as visually appealing. There are others that are vulgar beyond belief.

But, fine and handsome though many of these wines are, it will be clear from all that has gone before what the Bollinger attitude must have been towards the suggestion that they, too, should produce a premium-quality brand.

No, they must have said (and I can hear Madame saying it): we cannot change the proportion of black and white in our wine if we believe that the proportion we use at present is the right one. We cannot use only the *tête de cuvée* if we believe—as we do —that a sound champagne requires some of the juice of the *première cuvée* to give it backbone. In short, they would have summed it up: how can we make a better quality Bollinger than our vintage and our non-vintage? We already make the best wine we know how to make!

This, though, is what they decided to do. The decision was taken in 1961, when it was realized that Bollinger, too, was expected to produce a premium-quality wine.

From the reserves of undisgorged vintage wine, fine wines of great vintages, about ten or twelve years old, were chosen, and then disgorged for commercial distribution, presented under a special label giving the dates both of vintage and of disgorgement, and designated 'R.D.'—*récemment dégorgé*, or 'recently disgorged'.

Normally, as explained in chapter 6, both vintage and special cuvée Bollingers are taken off their sediments some four or five years after bottling, and even this is long by Champagne standards.

A longer spell even than that on its sediment means greater softness and mellowness in champagne—as those can bear witness who lunch or dine in the houses of hospitable champagne-makers and have venerable bottles, dating perhaps from the last century, brought up from the reserve bins and disgorged that morning for the honoured guest. How different from bottles that have aged *after* disgorgement—dark, lacking in bubble, perhaps *madérisé*![6]

One day in 1967 at Madame Bollinger's house in Ay I tasted the newly disgorged 1955—a wine that would normally have been disgorged seven or eight years earlier, in 1959 or 1960. And within the same week, at that splendid Paris restaurant, Lasserre, I was nobly treated to the Bollinger 1953 R.D., proudly labelled as having been disgorged as late as 25 January 1965. A little later, at home in England, I tasted the 1952 R.D., disgorged on 6 June 1967, and reported on it that, 'it marries its mellowness with the fresh dryness of late disgorging', though I found it, 'a shade lighter than I remember the 1953 R.D. as being'.

All three of these great wines were bland and mellow, to nose and to palate—later, in 1969, I tasted the 1959 R.D., disgorged at the end of 1968: it smelled old on first being poured out, but this 'old', almost *madérisé*, smell faded in the glass, and the wine became as winning as those others I had tasted previously.

---

[6] With excessive age, white wines lose their freshness and fragrance, and take on a musty taste and a brownish tinge reminiscent of madeira.

All these great wines showed a rather more subdued bubble than the ordinary vintage Bollinger would have shown, but they were still lively, and with true Bollinger character. Very much, indeed, to the English taste, for the English have always liked their French wines, whether claret or champagne, older than the French themselves do: Winston Churchill was typically English in this, as in so much else. Yet they showed, too, far greater youthful freshness than wines of the same years would have had, had they been disgorged—as they would normally have been—some half-a-dozen years earlier.

But the point is that the Bollinger premium-quality brand—'Bollinger's best', as I once described it in *The Observer*—is made in exactly the same way as any other Bollinger, vintage or non-vintage, because Bollinger do not know any other way, but is more bland and mellow because it has been kept longer on its lees, and more expensive only because capital has been tied up in it that much longer. It should appeal especially to the English taste for old champagne, and also to those—and let me be quite frank, and shock my Bollinger friends by saying that I am not one of them—who believe that champagne is a wine to serve throughout a meal. Though I am bound to admit that if I *were* to do so, this is the kind of wine I would choose, for its fullness of flavour and softness of style. If Bollinger ever decide to make a pink champagne, that would be more suitable still.

In the nature of things only a minute proportion of Bollinger's output—perhaps as little as 5 per cent—can be kept back like this for late disgorging. And only 1 per cent each year goes into double-magnums—as explained in chapter 6, Bollinger is the only firm to tackle the tricky business of fermenting in double-magnums, or jeroboams (other firms decant into nothing bigger than a magnum)—which would be my other choice as the very finest of all Bollinger wines, simply because, other things being equal, 'the bigger the bottle, the better the wine'. It has to do with the ratio of air to wine in the neck of the bottle.

Finally, a Bollinger champagne that is a good deal of an oddity—more than that, indeed: a museum piece—and a minute but important exception to all that has been said so far about the Bollinger insistence that champagne is essentially and necessarily made of a mixture of the juice of black and of white grapes: a *blanc et noir*.

Bollinger 'Vieilles Vignes Françaises' was first—and, so far, only—made in 1969. As explained in chapter 7, the house owns two small vineyards, one in Ay, one in Bouzy, still planted with pre-phylloxera vines—vines, that is, that withstood the great plague that destroyed virtually all the vineyards of France (and of most of Europe)—between the 1860s and the end of the century; although it will be remembered that it struck Champagne late—not until 1890—and was not fully mastered there, by grafting on to American stock, until after the First World War.

Here and there, though, a very few minute pockets of un-grafted pre-phylloxera vines still flourish: Bollinger's, so far as I can discover, are the only ones in Champagne. The vines are doubly freakish in that they are not only ungrafted, but far older than vines usually bear.

Grapes from these vines have always been put into the usual vintage or non-vintage blend of black and white. I am pleased to recall, and to record, that it was I who, on first being shown these two remarkable little vineyards in 1968, suggested that in some suitable year their yield should be kept separate, to be made into a pre-phylloxera vintage champagne—and what better vintage than 1969, the year of Madame Bollinger's seventieth birthday?

The grapes were gathered on 1 October 1969, the birthday eve, and in the spring of 1970 made about two thousand bottles, which ought to become collector's pieces when they are first listed in 1974. What makes them, as I have said, an exception to the Bollinger rule that only *blanc et noir* champagne is made, is that both little pocket-handkerchief vineyards are planted with the Pinot Noir: those couple of thousand bottles of Bollinger 'Vieilles Vignes Françaises' will contain that hitherto unknown wine, a Bollinger *blanc de noirs*.

It was tasted in December 1969, as soon as the first fermentation was completed, and Madame Bollinger was delighted with her anniversary wine. M. Christian Bizot wrote to me about it in terms of great enthusiasm: 'it is a shade dark in colour (in the old days champagne was not as clear gold as now); it is very round and complete; it is full without being heavy; it is elegant'.

M. Bizot went on to say that he was pretty sure that in 1974, when it was ready for the market, the Vieilles Vignes wine would show that the pre-phylloxera champagnes were different in style, as being fuller and rounder in body, than those of our own time. The only reservation I would make myself is that the proof would be more conclusive if there were white as well as black pre-phylloxera vines available. I have no doubt that M. Bizot is right, but one factor in the noticeable fullness of body of this wine is that it is a *blanc de noirs*, and we cannot be sure that it would be quite so full if there were an admixture of some 20 or 25 per cent of pre-phylloxera *white* grapes. That it would still be fuller than a present-day Bollinger I have no doubt, but *how* much fuller we cannot know. Meanwhile, it has been firmly decided that more of the pre-phylloxera wine will be made in good years.

There, then, is the whole Bollinger tally: Carte Blanche for South America; special cuvée (or non-vintage); vintage; R.D., which is vintage late-disgorged; once in a while perhaps, and perhaps once only, the vintage pre-phylloxera Bollinger Vieilles Vignes Françaises; and a mere thousand bottles a year—five hundred vintage and five hundred non-vintage, to be shared between France, Britain, the rest of Europe and the United States—of wine actually fermented in, not decanted into, double-magnums.

It will be understood why an appendix of this book is devoted to revealing where, in France and the main importing countries, the enthusiast can find Bollinger R.D. and Bollinger in jeroboams. (I fancy that those couple of thousand bottles of 1969 pre-phylloxera are all already spoken for.)

In Britain, it is easy to see whether the people at the next table in the restaurant are drinking non-vintage Bollinger: it is the only champagne without a 'neck-band' covering the edge of the gold foil. The red neck-band with gold lettering is reserved for the vintage Bollinger: in all countries other than Britain non-vintage carries a neck-band, too, but with 'Bollinger' in white instead of in gold.

The British label for non-vintage Bollinger is austerely dignified; black on white, even to the coat of arms that denotes the appointment of the Queen. The label for vintage carries the coat of arms in gold, the year in red, and a faint 'BRUT' in big letters but pale gold as a background. Like the wine in the bottle, the appearance of the label must be more expensive than the non-vintage: unlike the wine, its design is not as good—there is too much clutter of different type-faces and different inks.

Abroad, the 'BRUT' on the vintage labels is in heavier gold, and the word occurs on the non-vintage labels too, as it does not in Britain, but in pink instead of gold. Outside Britain, the label does not carry the royal arms.

Bottles of the R.D. look quite different from all the other Bollingers. They bear the name 'Bollinger' in neat black lettering on a small label of heavy gold paper, giving vintage year and disgorgement date (as it might be 'R.D. 1955: Degorgé le 18 Janvier 1968'), with the name and the disgorgement date again on the neck-band, in gold on black, and an explanatory back label, also in gold on black.

With this exception, below the bold roman-type BOLLINGER on the labels of every bottle of Bollinger, vintage and special cuvée, in every country of the world, is the original name of the firm in a flowing Victorian script—'Renaudin, Bollinger & Co., Ay-Champagne', a modest but rather agreeable memorial to the young Paul Renaudin who for a couple of years was the even younger first Bollinger's partner, a century and a half ago.

9. How to Drink Bollinger

I HAVE been entertained to dinner in my time by one of the great champagne families at its home in Reims, and not only had my food served to me on what looked very like gold plate, but the very distinguished wine of the house poured into splendid tulip-shaped glasses by Lalique, with the 'smiling angel' of Reims cathedral—already very familiar from picture postcards—modelled in high relief on the frosted, pearly-tinted glass. The wine tasted none the better for such splendour: indeed, it was the glasses upon which we felt obliged to compliment our hosts, whereas it should have been the champagne.

There would be more justification for Bollinger, as an Ay house, than for a family in Reims, to deploy such glasses, for René Lalique was born in Ay (in 1860: now, a quarter of a century after his death, his *art nouveau* pieces have become fashionable again). But Madame Bollinger and her colleagues and relatives live and entertain far more simply than this, and treat their equally well-bred wine with a less ostentatious—with a graver—dignity.

It is their custom—and I do not know of a better one—to serve their wine in tall glasses, tulip-shaped so that there is a fair amount of belly to hold a decent few mouthfuls of wine, but narrowing towards the top so that there is not too much immediate exposure of the surface of the wine to the air, causing a fairly rapid loss both of bubble and of fragrance.

It is for this reason that the tulip shape is preferable to the similarly elegant 'flute', the ancestry of which goes back to Gallo-Roman times and is the glass most often seen being used for champagne in French paintings and engravings of the eighteenth and nineteenth centuries. It is portrayed by English artists, too, from Hogarth, (though the same sort of eighteenth-century English glass is known to collectors as an ale-glass,)[1] to John Leech and his drawings of city gents at Epsom Downs for the *Punch* of the 1840s and '50s, where it is unmistakably champagne that it holds.

The flute is a handsome glass, but it offers a disappointingly small amount of wine to the drinker and a disproportionately large amount to the air.

The *coupe*, 'inverted ballet-skirt' glass, or *tazza*, is in its turn inferior to the flute, even if it were true that its origin is a set of Sèvres porcelain *tazze* modelled from the breasts of Marie-Antoinette (a photograph of one of these *tazze* most engagingly adorned the wrapper of Mr Patrick Forbes's book). In fact, alas, André Simon, who was profoundly scholarly in these matters, has shown that the *coupe* was designed and first made in England, specifically for champagne, in or about 1663, over a hundred years before Marie-Antoinette had any breasts to speak of.

Even so, the *coupe* did not come into general use in Britain and the United States until early Victorian times (Leech draws this kind of glass, too, for *Punch*) and, although by no means unknown in France, as some of Bertall's drawings for the champagne chapters in his *La Vigne* (1878) bear witness—though he

---

[1] It may well be ale that Tom Rakewell and his harlots are drinking from it at their 'Supper at the Rose', in plate 3 of *A Rake's Progress*.

draws rather more flutes than *coupes*[2]—it has never been whole-heartedly accepted there, and certainly not in Champagne. It lacks the elegance of the flute—indeed, the shape is ugly in itself, quite apart from its practicality or lack of it, because the bowl is too wide for the stem—and offers far more surface of wine to the air, thus allowing the bubbles to be dissipated far too quickly. The only notable wine-amateur of our time to defend it was old Warner Allen, who once wrote that he liked 'the generous expanse of golden wine it presents'. But what is precisely what is wrong with it! André Simon pointed out that it does not give the wine 'a fair chance to keep and show off its bubbles'. It is a vulgar, silly glass, fit only for the fancier confections of tinned fruit and factory-made ice-cream.

Next to the tulip-shaped glass, on a longish stem, I would recommend, and so I think would the *champenois* themselves, the rather squatter and rounder, but basically similar glass, on a shorter stem, that most English wine-drinkers choose for claret. I remember seeing a menu cover designed by 'Sem' for one of the very smart Bois de Boulogne restaurants of *la belle époque* reproduced as an illustration to an article by Mr James Laver, who knows so much about the history of fashion and of taste. Mr Laver observes that, 'the English custom of taking champagne in shallow saucer-like glasses has never found favour in France as can be seen from this illustration', which shows champagne being drunk from what I suppose we should call claret glasses. This is the sort of glass that holds a quarter of a bottle if filled absolutely to the brim, but is usually filled half-way, so that there is room to dip one's nose into the bouquet of the wine.

It is in the same way that Madame Bollinger and the other members of the family barely half-fill their similarly capacious tulip-shaped glasses, which are perfectly plain: there is no cutting and no engraving to obscure the enchanting sight of the bubbles steadily rising in the pale golden liquid. (Though I have it from André Simon that little stars engraved *inside* the glass will make the bubbles busier still. When I said that I could not understand why, M. Christian Bizot told me that the friction of the wine on

---

[2] His drawing on p. 141 shows both types of glass in use.

the minute rugosity in the surface of the glass releases its gas more freely. This sounds plausibly scientific, but leaves me little wiser than I was before.)

There may still be houses where the wine-glasses are the personal responsibility of the butler, and appear gleaming on the dinner-table, without ever a single smear or finger-mark or wisp of lint from a drying-up cloth in a couple of dozen of them.

Most households, though, have to do their best with hurried and amateur and too few hands and so, it seems—with less excuse—do many hotels and restaurants.

It is not only a matter of appearance, though a table of glittering glass looks splendid, whereas finger-marked glasses look squalid, but a matter, too, of taste. A whiff of the washing-up water will ruin a fine wine, as can the smell of a glass that is clinically clean, but been too long upside-down in a cupboard, catching and keeping a musty smell from the shelf it has been on.

The question now is, whether the newest washing-up devices make things easier for the wine-lover, as they certainly do for the washer-up, or whether they merely multiply the hazards in the way of tasting wine at its best, and seeing it at its prettiest.

Champagne is the severest test of all, for its bubble as well as its bouquet and flavour is at risk, and the directors of Mentzendorff, Bollinger's London agents, having noticed at many big parties that champagne 'fell dead' as soon as it was poured into the glass, held an experiment a couple of years ago.

They tried, with a selection of *grandes marques* champagne from Berry Brothers, four glasses that had been washed in detergent, and two washed in hot water, without the aid of a detergent. Of the detergent-washed glasses, one was allowed to drain dry; one was dried with a cloth; one was rinsed in hot water and drain-dried; and one was rinsed in hot water and cloth-dried.

According to the report on the experiment in the trade press, only one of those washed in detergent came through successfully—the glass that had been rinsed afterwards in hot water, and dried with a clean cloth. The other three all affected the 'bubble', but in varying degrees—the most damaging being the glass that had been simply drain-dried. (One brand of detergent proved to be not quite so immediately lethal as another, but both were so damaging that there is no point in naming brands.) The two glasses washed without a detergent also came through the test with flying colours.

It is clear that even a speck of dried detergent left in the glass has a harmful effect on champagne, but the same is true of soap, or of a drop of water. (Pour champagne into a perfectly clean but wet glass and see how the bubble dies.) My own experience with glasses washed with detergent in a washing-up machine that itself rinses in hot water as a final process is quite satisfactory. So use detergents, by all means, so long as you are sure that glasses are rinsed and cloth-dried afterwards: the same advice holds good for any other cleanser.

*   *   *

I have drunk Bollinger at my club from a silver tankard, and I am sure that Madame Bollinger would not have approved, old-established though the custom is in places of that sort. Metal, whether silver or pewter, gives the wine a taste quite different from what it has in a glass—not better and not worse, but different, and I think that a good *champenoise* like Madame would say that it is a taste alien to champagne, which the good Lord meant to be taken from glass. One has only to drink any fine wine, whether it is champagne or claret or hock, from a plastic cup or an enamel mug, to realize how important is the vessel from which one drinks, or the material of which it is made.

By the same token, I cannot believe that anyone who cares as deeply as Madame Bollinger does about the quality and character of the wine she makes could possibly approve of its being used as a component of Black Velvet, that mixture, otherwise known as Bismarck, of champagne and Guinness in equal quantities, that was Gerald du Maurier's favourite tipple and is said to be a sovereign cure for a hangover if taken at breakfast. Indeed, I think she would echo old George Saintsbury's, 'Between the flavours of stout and of champagne there is no possible *liaison*. The former simply overwhelms the latter; and all the wine does is to make the beer more intoxicating and more costly. Thus the thing is at once vicious and vulgar.'

I do not agree with this snobbish opinion of Black Velvet, to which I am very partial, but I would not use Bollinger.

On the other hand, I not only drink Buck's Fizz frequently at Buck's, but have once, at any rate, stood it there to M. Christian Bizot himself, Madame's nephew. If he disapproved, he concealed his disapproval admirably—or (as he is the firm's sales director and was drinking it in the company of partners in Mentzendorff's, its London agents) allowed it to be submerged in the pleasant realization that as the club has never used any champagne but Bollinger for its Buck's Fizz since Malachy McGarry, the then barman, introduced it in 1921, it must have sold a vast amount of Bollinger. (When I told him I had written this paragraph, he protested: he didn't disapprove at all, and he had no commercial considerations in mind when he described Buck's Fizz as 'most enjoyable'. I think he wanted to make sure that he would be asked again.)

This light and light-hearted drink consists of two parts of champagne to one of fresh orange juice, served very cold in a tall tulip-shaped glass. Pat Shanley, the present barman, who is McGarry's nephew and who has served Buck's Club for forty years, unbroken save for the war (when he was an Irish Guardsman, like his uncle), tells me that it does not always include the teaspoon of grenadine that Mr Patrick Forbes mentions—only when he decides, at the morning squeezings, that the oranges are not sweet enough. The same, or similar, delicious drink in France is *champagne-orange*, simply, and in Italy *mimosa* is made from Italian dry sparkling wine and fresh orange juice. I would not dream of using Bollinger for it at home, any more than I would use it for Black Velvet, but I am illogically proud of Buck's for its attitude of, 'the best is barely good enough'.[3]

No more, though, about champagne mixtures, of which

---

[3] They adopt a similar, and similarly admirable, attitude towards the other constituent of this delicious concoction at the Gritti Palace Hotel, Venice. The barman there, Giuseppe Fontana, once apologized as he handed me a *mimosa*, saying, 'Not so good, Mr Ray, I'm afraid, as when our own Italian oranges are in season. These are imported, and have come in refrigerated ships.' Not tinned, mind you, or frozen—simply *imported*, and not, therefore, up to the standard that the 'Gritti' sets itself.

Professor Saintsbury observed, more sensibly than when he pontificated about Black Velvet, that, 'if they are made of good wine they are wicked; if of bad, unpardonable'. Bollinger is too good to mix.

To the man who makes good champagne, and to the champagne-lover in general, the best apéritif in the world is champagne—by itself, and preferably a non-vintage, especially if a vintage wine is to follow with the meal, for it will be lighter than a vintage wine of the same *marque*. Not that a vintage champagne would be in the least out of place before a meal, if an older wine follows or if (as I prefer, myself) the wine with the meal is to be a claret or a burgundy. If there is to be a succession of champagnes, vintage should follow non-vintage, the older should follow the younger, the sweeter should follow the drier (I should like to taste the Bollinger Carte Blanche some time with fruit) and, with Bollinger, the R.D. should follow the vintage, for it is a fuller-flavoured wine, and—for those lucky enough eventually to possess any—the Vieilles Vignes Françaises should follow the R.D., for it will almost certainly be fuller still.

How should they be served, and at what temperature?

One of the many virtues of champagne is that it travels well: the gas imprisoned in the bottle enables it to do so. No matter how rough the journey, no matter what extremes of temperature on the way, once one has got the bottle home, it will be fit to drink as soon as it is cool enough. This is one reason why champagne is the superb picnic wine: an insulated bag will keep a bottle at the right temperature, but so, for that matter, will a thick overcoat of damp newspaper, if the bottle is clad in it as soon as it leaves the cellar.

I keep my own cellar at about 11.1°C (52°F) to 12.8°C (55°F), and at this temperature champagne is pleasantly cool to drink, though the bottle may be a little frisky in the opening. Ideally, it should be quite a bit cooler—Mr Patrick Forbes suggests between 6.6°C (44°F) and 8.8°C (48°F), and it is this latter figure that Madame Bollinger considers ideal. This is the temperature at which the wine is refreshingly cool without having had the taste and the bouquet muted by cold; the pressure of the gas in the bottle is also reduced, so that there should be no noisy explosion or unseemly loss of wine when it is opened. Half an hour in an ice-bucket, or rather longer in a refrigerator set at about 5°C (41°F) will get it right.

No doubt the 'pop' of champagne corks is a cheering sound, but the best way to open a bottle of champagne is to make sure that the cork does *not* pop. Remove the foil; undo the wire muzzle by twisting the loop anti-clockwise; hold the bottle at a slight angle above the horizontal, pointing away from the body; ease the cork out by holding it with the left hand, which is ready all the time to restrain any tendency for the cork to fly, while the right hand rotates the bottle gently clockwise. The cork should yield, and the gas escape, with a sigh, 'as from a well-contented woman'. I do not know where the late Youngman Carter found his admirably descriptive quotation.

Keep the bottle tilted at as near the same angle as possible as that at which you opened it. Pour a little of the wine into the first glass, where it will froth vigorously. While this subsides, you can begin the other glasses before going back to the first and so on back again, topping up as the froth subsides, but never more than two-thirds full.

Stubborn corks—and usually the bigger the bottle, the more stubborn: I have fought Homeric battles with magnums and, once, with a birthday-party methusaleh of Lanson—will yield to a pair of special tweezers, but these are hard to come by except in Champagne itself. A pair of strong thumbs can often force out a cork that will not yield to the gentle twisting of thumb and forefinger—but then the cork *will* pop. The best thing is to put the neck of the bottle in warm water, or under the hot tap for only a minute or so: the neck expands, the wax in the cork softens, and all should be well.

Smell the first few drops of wine, which will be poured into the host's, or the opener's glass, to see if there is any hint either of 'corkiness'—contamination by a diseased cork—or of *madérisation*, which is the, as it were, dark-brown or madeira-like smell of the champagne (or of any white wine) that has lived too long.

This reminds me of the stoppers that are available for keeping the bubble in the bottle for days after it has been opened, but not emptied. There is a one-lever type with rubber flanges that go inside the neck and can be tightened. This I find rather fiddly. And there is another, with two levers that press a rubber flange *on* to the top of the bottle. This is ideal, and can be picked up at any corner-shop in Reims or Epernay for a few shillings. Some British department stores have them, rather dearer, and some champagne houses, bless them, give them away free.

My own experience is that an opened bottle of champagne can be restoppered with one of these admirable devices and kept—upright—in the cellar or the refrigerator for a week or more, and still retain its fizz, or a good deal of it. Why mention of *madérisation* reminded me of the stopper, though, is that Madame Bollinger tells me she finds that champagne from a stoppered bottle that had been opened only a few hours earlier, even, is very slightly *madérisé*. And I can well believe her, for her palate has been her life as well as her livelihood for a generation, and this is precisely what a fine and a finely trained palate would certainly discern, where yours and mine, dear reader, would not.

All I know is that I would rather keep bottles of Bollinger in my cellar than half-bottles, or than the quarter-bottles that are produced for the American market, even if there are occasions when a bottle may have to be stoppered and finished later.

Finally, I had intended to write about—no, why should I use the word 'about'? I had intended to write *against* the swizzle-stick, or 'mosser'. But why should I? Before reaching this point, the reader, I hope, will have read my chapter on 'Bubble and Bottle', and will realize, without my labouring the point, why the bubble that has been so skilfully, so devotedly, so pain-stakingly and expensively put in, should not be swizzled out—not even by a gold mosser on a pearl-studded platinum chain from Bond Street, Fifth Avenue, or the Place Vendôme. A great champagne speaks to one in its bubbles, and who would silence so golden a voice?

*　　　*　　　*

Appendix I:

A Comparison of Climates

To give English readers an idea of the climate of the Champagne region, illustrating chapter 1, here is a comparison of the average monthly temperatures, monthly rainfall, and daily hours of sunshine of Reims and of Tunbridge Wells. The Kentish town has been chosen as being in the centre of a similar geographical and geological region, between the chalk North and South Downs, and as far as any town in this geographical position can be from the sea and its effects on average temperatures.

It will be seen that Reims is rather colder in the winter (by three degrees Fahrenheit in the day time in January, four degrees in the night time in December) and rather hotter in the summer (by five degrees in the day time in June, July and August). It has marginally, but only marginally, more sunshine over the year, and rather less rain.

COMPARATIVE AVERAGE TEMPERATURES
(degrees Centigrade, followed by Fahrenheit)

			REIMS	TUNBRIDGE WELLS
January	Day	maximum	4·4 (40)	6·1 (43)
	Night	minimum	− 1·1 (30)	0 (32)
February	Day	maximum	7·2 (45)	6·7 (44)
	Night	minimum	−0·6 (31)	0 (32)
March	Day	maximum	10 (50)	10·0 (50)
	Night	minimum	0·6 (33)	1·7 (35)
April	Day	maximum	15·6 (60)	13·4 (56)
	Night	minimum	4·4 (40)	3·3 (38)
May	Day	maximum	18·8 (66)	16·6 (62)
	Night	minimum	7·8 (46)	6·7 (44)
June	Day	maximum	22·8 (73)	20·0 (68)
	Night	minimum	11·1 (52)	9·4 (49)

Appendix I

			REIMS	TUNBRIDGE WELLS
July	Day	maximum	24·5 (76)	21·6 (71)
	Night	minimum	13·4 (56)	11·6 (53)
August	Day	maximum	24·5 (76)	21·6 (71)
	Night	minimum	12·2 (54)	11·6 (53)
September	Day	maximum	21·1 (70)	18·9 (66)
	Night	minimum	9·4 (49)	9·4 (49)
October	Day	maximum	14·4 (58)	14·4 (58)
	Night	minimum	6·1 (43)	6·1 (43)
November	Day	maximum	8·9 (48)	9·4 (49)
	Night	minimum	2·2 (36)	3·3 (38)
December	Day	maximum	5·0 (41)	7·2 (45)
	Night	minimum	− 0·6 (31)	1·1 (34)

COMPARATIVE AVERAGE HOURS OF DAILY SUNSHINE

	REIMS	TUNBRIDGE WELLS
January	2·1	1·8
February	3·1	2·5
March	5·0	4·1
April	5·7	5·6
May	6·9	6·7
June	7·3	7·5
July	7·1	6·8
August	6·5	6·3
September	5·5	5·0
October	3·9	3·6
November	2·0	2·0
December	1·6	1·6
Average:	4·725	4·458

COMPARATIVE AVERAGE MONTHLY RAINFALL
(inches)

	REIMS	TUNBRIDGE WELLS
January	1·8	3·0
February	1·5	2·3
March	1·9	2·0
April	1·9	2·2
May	2·1	2·1
June	2·1	1·7
July	2·6	2·3
August	2·3	2·4
September	1·7	2·2
October	2·6	3·3
November	2·3	3·6
December	2·3	3·2
Total for year:	25·1	30·3

Appendix II:

A Note on Vintage Years

A LIKING for old champagne is an English taste that the French do not share. Champagne-makers themselves will produce old bottles of famous years for honoured guests, but these have lain undisturbed and undisgorged in their own cellars: they are disgorged of their sediment at the last minute, and are fresher than bottles of the same year would be that have been bought in the ordinary way when young, already disgorged, and then left to acquire bottle-age in an English cellar, deepening in colour and losing bubble as the years go by. 'Full of body and character', say some, such as Winston Churchill, who doted on old Pol Roger. 'Like cold stewed tea', say others. Bollinger's R.D. is an attempt to meet both points of view, and a successful one: it has the body but has not lost the freshness. I am surprised that other houses have not also gone in for 'recently disgorged' oldish wines.

Mr Michael Broadbent of Christies tells me that there is enough demand in the auction-room for old champagnes to be snapped up whenever they are on offer, but not so much demand that prices rocket like those for old clarets: £3 or £4 will buy a vintage *grande marque* of twenty to thirty years old, which compares favourably—for those who like them—with the £2.50 asked for a current vintage champagne.

Amateurs of old champagne should know that Madame Bollinger, who has herself presided over the making of no fewer than thirteen vintages since she succeeded her husband as head of the firm, goes back to before any of them for the best she remembers drinking—to the 1928 and the 1934. The greater the wine, the longer its life, so long as it has been decently looked after, so it would be worth looking out for these years of Bollinger at Christies and at Sotheby's.

M. Christian Bizot's own report on the vintages shipped since the war is:

1945: rather vinous, well balanced and elegant.

1947: a fruity wine, generous, with great breed, straightforward, long lasting power.

1949: on the same lines as the 1947 but with less breed.

1952: very elegant and delicate, fine bouquet, not too fruity, a very charming wine.

1953: the reverse of the 1952, a great man, strong and straightforward, a wine for meals, its body marrying well with food.

1955: in the middle between 1952 and 1953, a wine to please all tastes, pleasant, amiable, delicate bouquet, fine body, a great wine.

1959: a big man, dry and fruity, on the heavy side, a difficult wine to make but which Bollinger made a success of.

1961: reminiscent of the 1955 with a touch more of vinosity, perfectly balanced and round, generous bouquet, a grand wine, an aristocrat (which will make a first-class R.D.).

1962: fruity and elegant, well balanced and round.

1964: a great thoroughbred, alert and lively, strong bodied and elegant at the same time, a long life ahead.

1966: not yet for sale but very promising.

It is natural to be sceptical when a producer praises his own product, and every wine here comes in for praise. But it must be remembered that these are vintage wines, which would not have been made had the vintages not assured quality above the average.

Of these I would nominate—and this is my own assessment—the 1947, the 1953, the 1959, and the 1961, as the wines to look for in the saleroom, the 1964 for lovers of old champagne to buy now and put away.

Appendix III:

Bollinger's Agents; and Where to Find the Great Bottles

BOLLINGER like to think of themselves as a firm that combines an old-fashioned air with a touch of style, a sort of dandified dignity. Over the years, they have picked appropriate agents—agents who reflect the 'style' of the house in the same way as the wine itself.

In France, for instance, M. Jean Verschave has been selling Bollinger for almost half a century, as have Mr Arne Tegner in Sweden, Mr J. Molbach-Thellefson in Finland, and Mr Ole Andersen in Denmark. Signor Gaetano Bandini and M. Hughes Nolet have built up the post-war Italian and Belgian markets, respectively, on exactly the same lines.

Mr J. H. Verlinden (Holland), Mr H. Bloch (Switzerland) and Mr Carl Tesdorff (Germany) have all helped to build up Bollinger's post-war sales in Europe, while in the New World Mr Van Sainsbury (Canada), Mr Harry Davidson (Colombia) and Mr Carl Rohl (Venezuela) have been notably successful.

But it is in the English-speaking world—easily the biggest market outside France itself for champagne in general, and proportionately even more so for Bollinger in particular—that we find the longest connections between agents and principals, and a very marked Bollinger 'style'.

In New England, the Pierce family have been the Bollinger agents since before the Spanish–American war; in the rest of the United States first Mr Richard Blum senr., and then his son, of Messrs Julius Wile Sons, agents for Bollinger since Repeal, have given it the same kind of prestige that it enjoys at home and in Britain.

It is in Britain, though, that we find the longest connection of all: it is as long ago as 1958 that Madame Bollinger was entertained by Messrs Ment-zendorff at the Savoy Hotel to celebrate the centenary of the two firms' association. For over a hundred years now, at least, the present that goes from London to the reigning head at Ay every Christmas has been a Stilton cheese. (Madame Bollinger betrays a certain amount of English influence in liking to accompany it with vintage port.)

The present directors, named in my introduction, carry on a tradition established in 1858 by the original Mentzendorff, and consolidated throughout the important decades for the champagne trade that lie between the Diamond Jubilee and the outbreak of the Second World War by the debonair Toby Folks, the Hon. Osbert Vesey of the Corps of Gentlemen-at-Arms, and Brigadier Brumell.

The present directors have instituted three sporting awards presented annually (usually by Madame Bollinger)—the Bollinger Trophy for the year's champion professional National Hunt jockey; the Bollinger Prize for the champion amateur rider, and the Bollinger Goblet for the *Daily Express* power-boat race round the Isle of Wight.

Since 1947 Mentzendorff have functioned from one of the four elegant eighteenth-century houses in tiny Pickering Place, earlier in date even than the shops of Berry Brothers the wine-merchants and Lock the hatters behind which the Place lies. The entrance to Pickering Place from St James's Street is so small and obscure that a taxi-driver once refused payment for taking Madame Bollinger there, on the grounds that a London taxi-driver should not have to be told by a French lady how to find a West-end address.

All sorts of legends have grown up around Pickering Place: that it was once a cockpit, and that it was the scene of the last duel to be fought in London. I know of no evidence for these stories. But there is a tablet in the dark, narrow passage leading to it, stating, under the Lone-Star device, that in the building forming the passage wall was the Legation for the Ministers from the Republic of Texas to the Court of St James, 1842–1845.

When I first knew it, a quarter of a century ago, Frank Hall, London's oldest licensed guide, then aged eighty-nine, used to sit on a soap-box at the entrance, a small man, wearing a fawn bowler, a different fancy waistcoat and bizarre walking-stick for every day of the week, and big antique—or antique-looking—rings on most fingers of each hand. One of the waistcoats, he said, was a present from Montagu Norman, and one of the walking-sticks, a handsome hand-made affair of Italian walnut, he told me was a present from Edward VII, who had seen him break his own there in a grating. What was Edward VII doing in Pickering Place? Frank winked a watery eye.

I was readier to believe his story that there used to be a time when the steward of the Conservative Club, then across the way, used to appear on the steps twice a week, catch Frank's eye and touch the brim of his bowler hat with a cautious forefinger: this was the signal that in the club's basement there awaited him, 'a good dinner, half a bottle of claret, and a fine cigar'. Probable enough, though it would have suited me better now, a quarter of a century later, if Frank had made it, not a half-bottle of claret, but an imperial pint of Bollinger.

*   *   *

From some of the agents mentioned I have extracted—it will be clear why from all that has gone before—lists of restaurants in Belgium, France, Italy and the United States that list Bollinger R.D., and the restaurants and wine-merchants in Britain that list the R.D. and also Bollinger in jeroboams. It will be understood that these lists are correct at the time of writing—late 1970—and that I cannot guarantee their accuracy indefinitely. But I hope that they may enable at any rate some of my readers to acquire the material by which to judge whether the opinions I have expressed about these bottles are justified.

BELGIUM
Restaurants listing Bollinger R.D. at the end of 1970:

Antwerp	La Rade
Brussels	Astrid 'Chez Pierrot'
	Bernard
	Brussels Grill Room
	Canterbury
	Carlton
	Cercle du Royal Automobile Club de Belgique
	Château-Ferme de Charles-Roy
	En Provence 'Chez Marius'
	La Cravache
	Taverne George III
	London Tavern
	Cercle Equestre La Métairie
	La Pergola
	Le Pré au Bois
	Rotisserie du Vieux Dieleghem
Fleurus	Auberge Maréchal Ney
Hamoir	Relais des Ardennes
Hertsberge	Maison de Caroline
Knokke le Zoute	Le Perchoir

Bollinger

BRITAIN

Restaurants and wine-merchants listing Bollinger R.D. at the end of 1970:

London restaurants	Annabel's
	Caprice
	Connaught Hotel
	Ecu de France
	Empress
	Grosvenor House
	Mirabelle
	Scott's
	Tiberio
	White House
London wine-merchants	Berry Bros & Rudd
	Christopher & Co
	Cockburn & Campbell
	Corney & Barrow
	Fortnum & Mason
	Greens
	Harrods
	Russell & McIver
	Stodart & Taylor
Country wine-merchants	Avery's of Bristol
	Vintage Wines Ltd of Nottingham

Restaurants and wine-merchants listing Bollinger in jeroboams at the end of 1970:

London restaurants	Café Royal
	Grosvenor House
	Hyde Park Hotel
	Inn on the Park
London wine-merchants	John Barker
	Berry Bros & Rudd
	Ellis & Co of Richmond
	Fortnum & Mason
	Harrods
	Robert Jackson
	Kettners
Country wine-merchants	Avery's of Bristol
	Owen & Son of Wilmslow

Appendix III

FRANCE
Restaurants listing Bollinger R.D. at the end of 1970:

Paris

Auberge de la Truite
La Camélia (Bougival)
Cabaret le Franc Pinot
Chez Denis
Chez Garin
Chez Joséphine
La Frégate
Lasserre
Ledoyen
La Marée
Maxim's
La Mère Michel
Le Munich
L'Orangerie
Le Pot au Feu
Le Quinze
Le Santal
Hôtel Terminus St Lazare
El Toro
La Truffière

ITALY
Restaurants listing Bollinger R.D. at the end of 1970:

Asiago	Linta Park Hotel
Biana di Ponte Dell'Olio	
Piacenza	Monte Santo
Bibione	Club Shany
Bologna	Hostaria del Sole
Bolzano	Taverna Goethe
Cala B.	Ringo Hotel
Clusone	Las Vegas
Esenta Lonato	Il Palazzino
Fie	Hotel Wolserhof
Lecco	Bar K 2
Macugnaga	Taverna del Rosa
Marina C.	Hotel Baia Cavoli

Bollinger

Milan	Jaguarfin
	Hotel Le Palme
	Riccione
	Savini
Ostia Lido	Hotel Satellite
Pecetto	Thera Club
Ponte di Brenta	Le Padovanelle
Procchio Elba	Hotel Renne
Riccione	Rist. Gino
Rome	Checco el Carrettiere
	Coriolano
	La Cuccagna
	Dal Bolognese
	Gigi Fazi
	Harry's Bar
	Sabatini
Tolmezzo	Alb. Roma
Turin	Chez Mario
	Dock Milano
Verona	Re Teodorico

UNITED STATES
Restaurants listing Bollinger R.D. at the end of 1970:

CALIFORNIA

Beverly Hills	Le Bistro
Los Angeles	Chasen's
	Scandia
Orange	Chez Cary
Palm Springs	Lord Fletcher
	Racquet Club
Pebble Beach	Del Monte Lodge
San Francisco	Alexis
	Blue Fox
	Hotel de France
	Le Club
	Paoli's

COLORADO

Aspen	The Copper Kettle
	The Red Onion
	The Paragon Parlor

Denver	Passport Restaurant
	Cherry Hills C.C.
Durango	Chez Louis
Scottsdale	Etienne's
	Chez Louis
Vail	Vail Village Inn

FLORIDA
Dania	Cordon Bleu
Fort Lauderdale	Dante's
	Down Under
Palm Beach	Petite Marmite
Pompano	Bayou South
St Petersburg	Vicca Rue

MINNESOTA
Minneapolis	Gay 90s
	200 Club

NEW JERSEY
Andover	Perona Farms
Englewood Cliffs	Sid Allen's
Tenafly	Clinton Inn
Union City	Swiss Town House

NEW YORK
New York City	Brussels Restaurant
	The Colony
	The Forum of the XII Caesars
	The Four Seasons
	Le Pavillon
	Maxwell's Plum
	The 21 Club
Rochester	Faculty Club
White Plains	Hunter's Lodge

TEXAS
Houston	The Houston Club

Appendix IV: The 1969 Echelle

Every year, at vintage time, the Comité issues its regulations: these include the *échelle* of prices referred to in Chapter 7.

VENDANGES 1969

Le Comité Interprofessionel du Vin de Champagne a déterminé ainsi qu'il suit les conditions dans lesquelles s'effectueront les vendanges en 1969.

MODALITÉS.—Pour bénéficier de l'appellation contrôlée «Champagne», les vins et moûts de la récolte 1969, outre qu'ils devront provenir de vignes répondant aux conditions d'âge, d'aire de production, de cépages, de tailles et de façons culturales déterminées par les lois et règlements en vigueur, devront:

(*a*) être obtenus par la mise en œuvre pour un **hectolitre** de moût, bouillage compris, de 150 kilogs de vendange mise en œuvre sur un pressoir appliquant les règles de pressurage prescrites par les lois et règlements en vigueur;

(*b*) provenir de raisins récoltés dans la limite de 12.000 kilogs à l'hectare;

(*c*) peser un minimum d'alcool en puissance de 9°5.

PRIX DU RAISIN.—Le barème ci-contre établit les prix obligatoires dans chaque cru conformément aux dispositions de l'arrêté préfectoral.

Le prix du raisin est fixé à 4 f. 14 le kilog pour les raisins récoltés dans les crus à 100%. Les prix des raisins récoltés dans les autres crus sont déterminés par application du pourcentage réel de chaque cru sur celui du cru à 100% (échelle 1945, modifiée).

A ce prix s'ajoutera une prime exceptionnelle et uniforme de 0 f. 10 par kilo.

En outre, il sera accordé une prime aux cepages nobles de 0 fr. 25 par kilo pour le pinot noir et pour le chardonnay.

Les conditions ci-dessus s'entendent pour des raisins sains, mûrs et marchands, c'est-à-dire épluchés s'il y a lieu et non oïdiés ni grêlés, et suivant les usages champenois pour moûts de vins, nus, départ, tous frais en sus.

Toutefois, dans le cas où pour des raisons d'ordre matériel, et pour ces seules raisons, certains vignerons ne pourraient livrer de tels raisins, les livraisons s'effectueront en 'triés' avec un abattement de 10% sur les prix et primes fixés pour les raisins sains. Ces livraisons en 'triés' pourront intervenir à la suite d'un accord entre les parties. Au cas de contestation le C.I.V.C. procédera à une enquête pour trancher le litige,

Sauf autorisation exceptionnelle accordée par le C.I.V.C. le logement des vendanges, moûts et vins en cercles ou en bouteilles en provenance de la propriété et non commercialisés est interdit dans des locaux appartenant à des Maisons de Champagne.

TRANSACTIONS À LA GOULOTTE.— Les transactions à la goulotte ne sont pas autorisées.

FRAIS DE PRESSURAGE ET COMMISSION.—Les frais de pressurage sont fixés comme suit quelle que soit la capacité du pressoir utilisé:

27 f. la pièce débourbée (cuvée ou taille);
24 f. la pièce non débourbée (cuvée ou taille);
29 f. la pièce de rebêche;

Frais d'entonnage (uniquement en futs) lorsque l'opération n'est pas effectuée par l'acheteur: 2 f. par pièce.

La Commission des Courtiers est fixée à 14 f. 45 la pièce. La Commission sur les ventes en bouteilles, sur lattes, sur pointe ou opérées est de 1%.

CONDITIONS DE PAIEMENT.—Les paiements se feront en quatre échéances égales, fixées au 20 Novembre 1969, 20 Février, 20 Mai et 5 Septembre 1970 sans faculté de report et sans intérêt.

D'entente entre les parties, et non à la volonté d'une seule, ils pourront être anticipés par l'acheteur moyennant un escompte de 0,70% par mois.

Toutefois, les achats d'un montant brut inférieur ou égal à 800 F, à condition que ce paiement représente le montant total de la récolte du vendeur, seront payés, en principe, en une seule échéance, sans escompte, le 20 Novembre 1969. Cependant, le vigneron aura la faculté de renoncer à cette clause et de suivre le régime commun.

Tout retard dans le paiement d'une échéance fera courir d'office, au bénéfice du vendeur, un intérêt de 0,70% par mois sur les sommes dues, qui n'en restent pas moins exigibles.

VERSEMENT DE 8%.—Les Négociants ayant souscrit un engagement d'approvisionnement devront verser à un compte spécial ouvert par le C.I.V.C. et géré par ce dernier une somme égale à 8% de la valeur de leurs achats.

(*Suite en dernière page*)

Crus	Echelle %	Prix du Kilog		Crus	Echelle %	Prix du Kilog
Ambonnay	100	4.140		Chambrecy	81	3.353
Avenay	93	3.850		Chamery	88	3.643
Avize............	100	4.140		Champillon.......	93	3.850
Ay-Champagne ...	100	4.140		Champlat-Bouja-		
Barbonne-Fayel				court	81	3.353
noirs	82	3.395		Champvoisy	82	3.395
blancs	85	3.519		Châtillon-sur-		
Baslieux-sous-				Marne	82	3.395
Châtillon.......	81	3.353		Chaumuzy	81	3.353
Baye	85	3.519		Chavot-Courcourt		
Beaumont-sur-				noirs	87	3.602
Vesle	100	4.140		blancs	88	3.643
Beaunay	85	3.519		Chenay	82	3.395
Belval-sous-				Chigny-les-Roses		
Châtillon	81	3.353		noirs	94	3.892
Bergères-les-Vertus				blancs	86	3.560
noirs	90	3.726		Chouilly ...noirs	90	3.726
blancs	93	3.850		blancs	95	3.933
Berru	82	3.395		Coizard-Joches ..	85	3.519
Bethon ...noirs	82	3.395		Coligny	85	3.519
blancs	85	3.519		Comblizy	81	3.353
Billy-le-Grand	90	3.726		Congy	85	3.519
Binson-Orquigny .	83	3.436		Cormicy	81	3.353
Bisseuil	93	3.850		Cormoyeux.......	83	3.436
Bligny	81	3.353		Coulommes-la-		
Bouilly	86	3.560		Montagne	89	3.685
Bouleuse	80	3.312		Courcelles-Sapi-		
Boursault	81	3.353		court	80	3.312
Bouzy	100	4.140		Courjeonnet	85	3.519
Branscourt	86	3.560		Courmas	87	3.602
Breuil(le).........	81	3.353		Courtagnon	80	3.312
Brimont	81	3.353		Courthiézy	81	3.353
Brouillet	86	3.560		Cramant	100	4.140
Broyes	85	3.519		Crugny	86	3.560
Brugny-Vaudan-				Cuchery	81	3.353
court	86	3.560		Cuis ......noirs	90	3.726
Cauroy-lès-				blancs	95	3.933
Hermonville....	81	3.353		Cuisles...........	82	3.395
La Celle-sous-				Cumières........	90	3.726
Chantemerle				Damery ...noirs	85	3.519
noirs	82	3.395		blancs	86	3.560
blancs	85	3.519		Dizy	95	3.933
Cernay-les-Reims .	85	3.519		Dormans (Try,		
Cerseuil	82	3.395		Vassy, Vassieux,		
Chalons-sur-Vesle	82	3.395		Chavenay)	81	3.353

Crus	Echelle %	Prix du Kilog		Crus	Echelle %	Prix du Kilog
Ecueil	90	3.726		Mesnil-sur-Oger		
Epernay	88	3.643		(le)	99	4.099
Etoges	85	3.519		Montbré	94	3.892
Etrechy ...noirs	87	3.602		Monthelon	88	3.643
blancs	90	3.726		Montigny-sous-		
Faverolles	86	3.560		Châtillon.......	83	3.436
Fèrebrianges......	85	3.519		Morangis	84	3.478
Festigny	81	3.353		Moslins	82	3.395
Fleury-la-Rivière				Moussy	88	3.643
noirs	83	3.436		Mutigny	93	3.850
blancs	83	3.436		Nesle-le-Repons...	81	3.353
Fontaine-Denis				Neuville-aux-		
noirs	82	3.395		Larris (la)	81	3.353
blancs	85	3.519		Nogent-l'Abbesse	87	3.602
Germigny	85	3.519		Œuilly...........	81	3.353
Givry-les-Loisy ...	85	3.519		Oger	99	4.099
Grauves ..noirs	90	3.726		Oiry.............	99	4.099
blancs	93	3.850		Olizy-Violaine	82	3.395
Gueux	85	3.519		Ormes	80	3.312
Hautvillers	90	3.726		Oyes	85	3.519
Hermonville	82	3.395		Pargny-les-Reims..	89	3.685
Hourges	86	3.560		Passy-Grigny	82	3.395
Janvry	85	3.519		Pévy	81	3.353
Jonquery	82	3.395		Pierry	90	3.726
Jouy-les-Reims ...	89	3.685		Poilly............	81	3.353
Lagery...........	86	3.560		Port-à-Binson	82	3.395
Leuvrigny........	82	3.395		Pouillon	82	3.395
Loisy-en-Brie	85	3.519		Pourcy	82	3.395
Louvois	100	4.140		Prouilly..........	82	3.395
Ludes ....noirs	94	3.892		Puisieulx	100	4.140
blancs	86	3.560		Reims (Lot Brisset)	88	3.643
Mailly-Champagne				Reuil	83	3.436
noirs	100	4.140		Rilly-la-Montagne .	94	3.892
blancs	86	3.560		Romery	83	3.436
Mancy ....noirs	86	3.560		Rosnay	81	3.353
blancs	88	3.643		Sacy	90	3.726
Mardeuil	82	3.395		Sainte-Euphraise ..	86	3.560
Mareuil-le-Port ...	82	3.395		Sainte-Gemme ...	82	3.395
Mareuil-sur-Ay ...	98	4.057		Saint-Martin		
Marfaux	82	3.395		d'Ablois	86	3.560
Merfy	82	3.395		St-Thierry		
Mery-Premecy	80	3.312		basses vignes	87	3.602
Mesneux (les)	90	3.726		Sarcy	81	3.353
Mesnil-le-Hutier				Saudoy ....noirs	82	3.395
(le)	82	3.395		blancs	85	3.519

Crus	Echelle %	Prix du Kilog
Savigny-sur-Ardre	86	3.560
Sermiers	88	3.643
Serzy-et-Prin	86	3.560
Sézanne ...noirs	82	3.395
blancs	85	3.519
Sillery	100	4.140
Soilly	81	3.353
Soulières	85	3.519
Taissy	94	3.892
Talus-Saint-Prix...	85	3.519
Tauxières	99	4.099
Thil	82	3.395
Toulon-la-Montagne	85	3.519
Tours-sur-Marne noirs	100	4.140
blancs	90	3.726
Tramery ...noirs	86	3.560
blancs	86	3.560
Trépail	90	3.726
Treslon	86	3.560
Trigny...........	82	3.395
Trois-Puits	94	3.892
Troissy	81	3.353
Unchair	86	3.560
Vandeuil	86	3.560
Vandières	82	3.395
Vauciennes	81	3.353
Vaudemanges.....	90	3.726
Venteuil	85	3.519
Verneuil	82	3.395
Vert-la-Gravelle...	85	3.519
Vertus	93	3.850
Verzenay...noirs	100	4.140
blancs	86	3.560
Verzy ....noirs	99	4.099
blancs	86	3.560
Villedommange ..	90	3.726

Crus	Echelle %	Prix du Kilog
Ville-en-Tardenois	79	3.271
Villeneuve-Renneville	93	3.850
Villers-Allerand ..	90	3.726
Villers-Franqueux	82	3.395
Villers-Marmery ..	90	3.726
Villers-sous-Châtillon.......	83	3.436
Villevenard.......	85	3.519
Vinay	86	3.560
Vincelles	83	3.436
Vindey ....noirs	82	3.395
blancs	85	3.519
Vrigny	89	3.685
Marne (crus non cotés)	75	3.105

AISNE

Canton de Condé-en-Brie

	Echelle %	Prix du Kilog
Barzy-sur-Marne ..	82	3.395
Passy-sur-Marne ..	82	3.395
Trélou-sur-Marne ..	82	3.395
Beaulne-en-Brie ..	81	3.353
Aisne (moins les communes ci-dessus du Canton de Condé-en-Brie)........	75	3.105

AUBE

	Echelle %	Prix du Kilog
Tous les crus de l'Aube	75	3.105

Cotisations et retenues

Chaque transaction intervenant entre le commerce et la propriété lors des vendanges, donnera lieu à la per-ception d'un droit de 0,90% du prix de vente, destiné au C.I.V.C.

Ce droit, dont le coût sera sup-porté à raison de 0,60% par les vendeurs et 0,30% par les acheteurs de la vendange, sera comtabilisé par les acheteurs, et versé par eux au Comité interprofessionnel du Vin de Champagne, par parts égales, quinze jours après chacune des échéances fixées pour le paiement de la vendange. La part de ce droit incombant au vendeur sera obligatoirement mentionnée sur le bon d'achat prescrit.

Pour la vendange conservée par les Récoltants qu'ils soient Manipulants ou non, ce droit de 0,90% sera entièrement supporté par les intéressés. Son montant (calculé sur la valeur que l'échelle des crus détermine dans le cru de l'intéressé pour les vins qu'il conserve), sera versé par lui au C.I.V.C., comme prévu ci-dessus, quinze jours après chacune des échéances fixées pour le paiement de la vendange.

Les maisons propriétaires de vignobles paieront de leur côté une cotisation de 0,60% sur la valeur de leur récolte.

Les Négociants acheteurs pourront être requis de collecter pour le compte du C.I.V.C., les cotisations dues par leurs vendeurs, pour des vendanges conservées ou des expéditions, et non acquitées dans les délais prescrits.

Parallèlement, le C.I.V.C. recevra, pour le compte du Syndicat Général des Vignerons, les cotisations de ses adhérents fixées à o f. 25 par 100 kilogs de raisins.

DISPOSITIONS COMPLÉMENTAIRES

Aucune transaction entre propriétaires récoltants et négociants ne pourra se faire sans que soit remis au livreur un bon provisoire tiré d'un carnet à souche et portant obligatoirement:

— la quantité achetée,
— le nom du livreur,
— le nom de l'acheteur,
— éventuellement, le nom du Courtier lorsque l'acheteur confie à un intermédiaire le soin d'effectuer ses achats.
— la qualité des raisins (épluchés ou non), (avec ou sans prime).
— le numéro du bon d'achat.

En fin de vendange, ces bons provisoires seront récapitulés en bons de livraison définitifs établis en quatre exemplaires: l'un de ces quatre exemplaires est destiné à l'acheteur, le deuxième au vendeur, le troisième au mandataire éventuel, le quatrième restant à la souche, sera remis au C.I.V.C. aux fins de contrôle.

Demeurent interdites: Les ventes à des personnes physiques ou morales non porteuses de carte de Manipulant, de raisins ou moûts pouvant revendiquer l'appellation «Champagne».

- *Date d'ouverture des vendanges:* *1er Octobre 1969*
- *Date de fin des vendanges:* *8 Novembre 1969*
- *Dépot des carnets de pressoirs:* *au plus tard le 10 Novembre 1969*
- *Déclarations de récolte:* *cloture des registres le 12 Novembre 1969*

Select Bibliography

H. WARNER ALLEN, *The Wines of France*, London, 1924.
—, *White Wines and Cognac*, London, 1952. (Not so careful with his facts as one might feel entitled to expect from the First in Mods, or the parade of classical scholarship in his *A History of Wine*, 1961, but he was an enthusiastic amateur of wine, and an eye-witness of the Ay riots of 1911.)

BERTALL, *La Vigne*, Paris, 1878. (See note under list of illustrations.)

PATRICK FORBES, *Champagne*, London, 1967. (It will be clear to the reader how much I have leaned on this encyclopaedic work: it is indispensable.)

R. GANDILHON, *Naissance du Champagne*, Paris, 1968.

YVES GANDON, *Champagne*, Neuchatel, 1958. (Personal and discursive about the wine and the countryside: splendid photographs of scenery and of cellar and vineyard processes.)

JULES GUYOT, *Etudes des Vignobles de France*, volume III. Paris, 1868. (Useful on vineyard practice in Champagne's pre-phylloxera period.)

MAURICE HOLLANDE, *Sur les Routes de Champagne*, Reims, n.d. (Helpful factual guide to its towns and villages, churches and great houses.)

EDWARD HYAMS, *Vin: the Wine Country of France*, London, 1959.
—, *Dionysus: a Social History of the Wine Vine*, 1965. (Mr Hyams does not care very much for champagne, but no living Englishman knows more about the history of the vine or about the effects of climate and microclimate on wine: he is a scholar and a wine-grower.)

HUGH JOHNSON, *Wine*, paperback edition, London, 1968. (Written when the author was still in his twenties, there is an engaging enthusiasm in the pages on champagne, and some forthright expressions of opinion on styles and qualities.)

J. NOLLEVALLE, *L'Agitation dans la Vignoble Champenois*, special issue of *La Champagne Viticole*, January, 1961. (The only full account I have come across of the disturbances of 1910–1911, for which I also consulted files of *The Times*, *Morning Post* and *Illustrated London News*.)

ANDRÉ SIMON, *History of the Champagne Trade in England*, London, 1905.
—, *The Noble Grapes and the Great Wines of France*, London, 1957.
—, *The History of Champagne*, London, 1962.

Select Bibliography

HENRY VIZETELLY, *A History of Champagne*, London, 1882. (Vizetelly was a sound reporter, widely read, and with a well-stocked mind. Until Mr Forbes came along, this was the best and most comprehensive book on champagne, and it is still informative and eminently readable.)

WILLIAM YOUNGER, *Gods, Men and Wine*, London, 1966. (A vast history of wine from the earliest days, exquisitely written, it places champagne in its historical perspective.)

Index

Index